CHRISTIANITY
Among the Religions
of the World

CHRISTIANITY
Among the Religions of the World

ARNOLD TOYNBEE

CHARLES SCRIBNER'S SONS * NEW YORK

This book is dedicated to

THE ANDOVER NEWTON THEOLOGICAL SCHOOL,
THE EPISCOPAL THEOLOGICAL SCHOOL,
AND
UNION THEOLOGICAL SEMINARY,

under whose auspices I had the honor of giving these Hewett Lectures.

I am grateful for the hospitality with which my wife and I were received, and for the discussion that I had with members of the three schools.

PREFACE

This book is a discussion of the attitudes of Christians toward the followers of the other great living religions. It examines what this attitude is, and what it should be. The writer also tries to survey what the position of Christianity and the other religions is in the setting of the modern world and in face of the resurgence of another religion which is an old one and a bad one: our worship of ourselves in the plural in the shape of collective human power.

On one side of the Iron Curtain this common adversary of all the higher religions takes the form of Communism; on the other side it takes the form of Nationalism. At bottom, Nationalism and Communism are variations of the same perverse theme: man's self-centered worship of himself.

The writer does not expect to see the historic higher religions coalesce into a single religion, and he does not advocate this; but he does put the question whether, in the face of such a formidable and evil opponent, the higher religions ought not now to stand together in preaching the supremely important negative belief that is common to them all. They all believe that man is not the highest spiritual presence in the universe. This belief is worth fighting for. If we lose it, we shall go to perdition. For only humility can save mankind from destroying himself.

While I have been revising these lectures for publication, I have had the pleasure of being constantly reminded of the visit to the United States, in the fall of 1955, during which the lectures were delivered. This gives me an opportunity to express my gratitude to the presidents, faculties, and students of the three seminaries which administer the Hewett Foundation. My wife and I shall always remember the kindness and hospitality with which we were received, and the keenness, sincerity, and forbearance shown in the discussions by which the lectures were followed.

ARNOLD TOYNBEE

THE INTERNATIONAL HOUSE OF JAPAN
TOKYO

19 October, 1956

CONTENTS

I

What Are the Criteria for Comparisons between Religions?

THIS book will deal with the subject of "Christianity and the non-Christian Faiths in the Contemporary World," and there can be no doubt that this subject is a very important one. Perhaps our agreement that it is important is the only non-controversial aspect of it. I am conscious that, for the rest, it is controversial, partly just because it is of such great concern to all of us today. While I am writing, I am aware that every one of the suggestions that I make may give occasion for perhaps half-a-dozen counter-suggestions. I am also conscious that I have never been a missionary, and that I have no direct personal experience of the field of contact between Christianity and any of the other great living faiths. I am also not a theologian, and therefore I shall probably say many things that will seem either very crude and elementary, or very fundamentally mistaken to people who have been trained in theology. I write as an historian with a Christian upbringing and background, and am therefore, from the point of view of my readers, an amateur.

In this initial chapter I want to discuss what, I think,

must be the first subject on one's agenda when one is trying to open up this general topic. What are the criteria, the tests, the bases, for comparing religions with one another at all? Unless one can find some basis for comparison, one cannot find one's way into the subject. Now the higher religions have been founded by teachers who have claimed to be mouthpieces of an authoritative revelation of the truth about ultimate reality. And so I suppose that, if any of the followers of any of the living higher religions were asked to judge between their own religion and the other great religions, their first impulse would be to compare their respective beliefs.

You may ask: Does that apply to Hinduism? This question arises because I am going to assume that Hinduism is one of the living higher religions. Is Hinduism a religion that has historic founders and that bases itself on beliefs? Is not Hinduism founded above all on rites and practices, and are not its beliefs based on tradition rather than on revelation? The answer to these questions depends, no doubt, on the sense in which one takes Hinduism. If one takes Hinduism as being the living Hindu religion of today, and traces that back as far as one can without meeting with any break in continuity, I think one will find Hinduism rising in about the eighth or ninth century of the Christian Era—and not earlier than that—as a conscious reaction against Buddhism. And I think one will find that it has founders who have expressed its difference from Buddhism in intellectual terms, in terms of belief. The very names of the Hindu sects—the dualist, the non-dualist, the extreme dualist, the mitigated dualist —show that Hinduism, too, has expressed itself in intellectual terms, at any rate in the minds of the most articulate exponents of the post-Buddhaic form of the Hindu religion.

But what about Buddhism? It is recorded of the Buddha that, whenever any of His disciples asked Him to expound the metaphysical basis of His system, He always refused to discuss metaphysics, on the ground that what He was urging upon His disciples was that they should enter upon a strenuous course of self-discipline leading to the extinction of desire, and that it was human frailty that was inducing them to turn aside from that difficult path of action towards intellectual speculation. The Buddha was not going to let them out through this easy door of escape. Yet even Buddhism would insist on the importance of its beliefs about the practical matters which are the starting-point of the Buddha's prescription for self-release from suffering. It would insist on the beliefs prescribed by the Buddha about the cause of suffering and the means of release from it. And I think that the followers of all the other living higher religions would be likely to take metaphysical beliefs as their touchstones when they first approached this question of what the tests ought to be in trying to make a comparison between religions.

At the same time, this notion of beliefs is surely a very

recent innovation in the long history of religion. If one looks into its origin, one finds, I believe, that it has come to the higher religions from the philosophers. That is very obvious in the case of the Indian group of religions. Buddhism arose as one philosophical school in a debate among a number of Indian philosophies; and Hinduism in its present form arose as a philosophical or theological reaction against the philosophical position of Buddhism. It is true that Christianity and Islam did not originate, as the religions of the Indian group did, in philosophical surroundings, or in a philosophical atmosphere. They originated, both of them, among people who were rather far removed from a philosophical education or a philosophical approach to the problems of life. Yet the exposition of Christianity in the Greek language (and Christianity was expounded in the Greek language at a very early stage of its history) implicated Christianity in Greek philosophy, because, by the first century of the Christian Era, the Greek language was long since imbued with a Greek philosophical vocabulary, conveying Greek philosophical ideas. And I think that, as soon as the Epistles and the Gospels were written, and written in Greek, Christianity was committed to expressing itself sooner or later in terms of Greek philosophy. At any rate, as it made its way through the Graeco-Roman world and evangelized one class of society after another, grappling last of all with the sophisticated educated minority of that society, it found itself constrained to express its beliefs in strict terms of Greek philosophy. So did Islam, following at Christianity's heels, because Islam came of age in a region—Syria, Egypt, and Mesopotamia—that, for about a thousand years, had been under the influence of Greek culture. In this environment Islam, like Christianity before it, came to terms with Greek philosophy and expressed its beliefs in Greek philosophical terminology.

The point that I am trying to make is that the equation of religion with belief is rather recent. After all, in both India and Greece, the philosophical approach to the problems of life is hardly older than the seventh or the sixth century before the beginning of the Christian Era; and that is a very recent date even in the brief history of Civilization, not to speak of the far longer history of Man. Even the beliefs of the older school of Buddhism— the school that deprecated metaphysics and sought to confine the discussion of beliefs to those beliefs that are of practical utility for the conduct of life and for the fulfillment of the Buddha's practical aim of the extinction of desire—even those utilitarian beliefs seem sophisticated and self-conscious when compared with the attitude of primitive religion. Primitive religion is concerned, I take it, not at all with beliefs, but wholly with practice. And the beliefs that the higher religions have imported from previous philosophies are not ends in themselves. Perhaps that is a controversial thing to say. It might be more accurate to say that the beliefs of the higher religions are inseparable from practice, or rather that, when any adherent of any of the higher religions does separate his beliefs from his practice, and does not attempt to carry out in practice any part of what he believes, this is felt, and rightly felt, to be a scandal. A profession of beliefs without practice is rightly felt to be hypocritical. I should say that the higher religions differ from primitive religions in underpinning the practice that they inculcate with a foundation of beliefs, but I would also suggest that, for the higher religions too, practice is the ultimate end.

Ought we, then, to look to practice in order to find our tests or criteria for comparing the different higher religions with one another? If one looks to practice, there are, I should say, two alternative main ways in which the practice of religion can be appraised. One way would be to try to measure how far the practice of a particular religion falls short of that same religion's ideals and precepts and professions. Another way would be to leave ideals and professions out of account for the sake of the argument, and to try to compare the actual conduct of the adherents of one religion with the actual conduct of the adherents of other religions. But as soon as one attempts to apply either of these methods of appraisal, one finds that each of them presents some rather serious pitfalls. Let us take first the test of the extent of the discrepancy between practice and profession. On this test, Islam would seem, at first sight, to come off best of all the living higher religions. It is, I suppose, a fact that a greater percentage of professing Muslims live up to their professions than is to be found in any other living religious communion. But the moment we have made this observation, we see that the reason for the fact is because Islam has set its standards at a "ceiling" that is more or less attainable by ordinary people. I need not go into the historical causes of that. They lie partly in the character and the career of the prophet Muhammad and partly in the political and social and cultural conditions of the particular part of the pagan world in which he carried out his ministry. But, as Christians see it, anyway, the commandments laid on all members of the Christian Church are more exacting than the commandments laid on all Muslims.

Moreover, beyond the Christian commandments, there are Christian precepts that are not obligatory but are counsels of perfection for a spiritually ambitious minority. And then there is another group of religions which carries that tendency further. I am thinking of the older school of Buddhism, I am thinking of Manichaeism, and I am thinking of the Cathar heresy, which in the early Middle Ages spread from the Eastern Orthodox Christian World to Western Christendom. In the religions of that class, the commandments are about as exacting as the Christian precepts, with the consequence that, in these other communions—the primitive Buddhist, the Manichaean, the Cathar—full church membership has been confined to a small spiritual elite. The majority of the faithful, like the majority of Mankind, have to live the life of the world; so they have been necessarily kept down to the status of proselytes who have remained, so to speak, second-class citizens of their church. Therefore, in comparing practice with precepts, it is important to distinguish precepts addressed to ordinary people from precepts addressed to an elite. But, when we do draw this very necessary distinction, we find that the discrepancy between practice and profession does not, after all, give us any clear criteria for a comparison between religions. Islam, too, has its monastic orders and its mystical sects who aspire to a spiritual level that is not obligatory for ordinary Muslims. In fact, every higher religion has several "storeys" or "ceilings" for practice: the lowest storey for ordinary people, the highest storey for saints, and perhaps one or more storeys in between for people who are half-way up the ladder of spiritual attainment. And when one compares religions, as one should, not by equating the highest storey of one with the lowest storey of another, but storey for storey, then the differences of level do not seem so very striking.

Then what about comparing the actual conduct of the followers of the different religions? The first question that arises here is: Whose conduct in each church? We are immediately brought back to the same question: Whom are we to take as our sample? Ordinary people? Or the spiritual elite? And, if there are people of such different degrees of spiritual attainment, if the gamut of spiritual attainment is very wide—and it is rather wide, I think, in every religious community—is there any sense in trying to strike, so to speak, a spiritual average of this or that church or religious community, an average of its adherents' spiritual stature? If one is concerned with physical stature, to strike an average is, of course, often a very useful operation. If a government wishes to raise an army and tells the army clothing department to provide the necessary amount of cloth, it is very useful to know the average physical stature of the adult male section of that country's population; for then a simple sum will give you the number of millions of square yards of cloth that you will need for making uniforms. But it does not make sense to apply that simile to spiritual stature. I think, myself, that it makes nonsense. There is really no meaning in striking a spiritual average. Though most of our words for spiritual things are derived from our vocabulary for physical things, owing to the infirmity of human minds and the poverty of human language, I think that in this case the physical analogy does not really make sense. In twentieth-century Tibet, for example, or in eighteenth-century Naples, one finds saints who would be spiritually eminent at any time or place living among a population whose religious practice is not only primitive but crude or even, from our point of view, benighted. When I speak of eighteenth-century Naples, I have in mind Saint Alfonso Liguori, the founder of the Redemptorist Order, whose home was a city surrounded by a peasantry living at what we, I suppose, should call a very low level of spiritual life. Yet this saint would not have felt himself sundered from his benighted fellow Christians in the Kingdom of Naples. How are we to appraise the religious practice of a community in which the religious gamut is as wide as that?

Moreover, even if it did make sense to try to strike an average of spiritual practice, a comparison between the practices of different societies would be made difficult by a difference on which I have touched already in discussing the relation of the several higher religions to secular society. To apply the notion of the division between church and state to Islam would run counter to the whole Islamic concept of religion and way of life; and, as we know, this has caused great difficulty in our time in Islamic countries that have tried to adopt Western, and therefore, at bottom, Western Christian, constitutions and social systems. In Hinduism, things like the institution of caste implicate the Hindu religion in the Hindu way of life. When you come to Christianity and to the Mahayanian or northern school of Buddhism, which is now the prevalent form of Buddhism in Eastern Asia, one might say that those two religions are *in* a secular society but not *of* it. When you come to the religions with an inner circle of what the Manichaeans and the Cathars call the "perfect," or what in the older school of Buddhism is virtually an order of monks, you find that that inner circle, who constitute the true church, are almost completely withdrawn from secular society. So a basis for comparison is very difficult to obtain.

Let us, for a moment, limit our attention to Christendom and try to make a very cursory survey of the practice of different provinces of Christendom at the present day. We shall arrive at what may seem, at first sight, to be a rather disconcerting result. In some parts of Christendom, during the last two hundred and fifty years or thereabouts, there has been a progressive repudiation of Christian belief. What has been the relation between the state of Christian belief and the state of Christian practice in different parts of the modern Christian world? I think one might get the impression that today the percentage of professing church members and the level of ordinary people's standards of conduct vary almost inversely with one another when measured by the demands of Christianity—the demands made, not on the elite, but on ordinary people. In what part of Christendom today should we find the percentage of professed agnostics and atheists lowest? Looking round the map, I think we should probably put our finger on the Transcaucasian province of Abkhazia, where, I imagine, few people have heard of such a thing as agnosticism or atheism. The percentage would also certainly be lower than the average in the toe of Italy, Calabria. The percentage would be high, perhaps at its highest, in the Scandinavian countries. And yet, when one makes the comparison of conduct, judged by Christian standards, the Scandinavian countries would, of course, stand rather near the top of our list, and Abkhazia would probably stand rather near the bottom, while Calabria would probably stand nearer to Abkhazia than it would to Scandinavia. So it might look as if the provinces of Christendom which are the most Christian in conduct are those that have gone the farthest in repudiating the profession of Christianity.

Are we then to infer that the repudiation of traditional Christian belief is to be equated with intellectual enlightenment, and that intellectual enlightenment automatically brings moral improvement with it? Before we jump to that disconcerting conclusion, we must, of course, extend our survey to other provinces of Christendom which I have not yet brought into view. Between Calabria and Scandinavia there lie Italy and Germany, and, east of Germany, then lies Russia. Does our apparent law that the profession of Christian beliefs and the practice of Christian virtues vary inversely with one another hold good in contemporary Italy, Germany, and Russia, too? No, in Communist Russia and Fascist Italy and Nazi Germany, we have seen, in our lifetime, power being seized by an ex-Christian minority who have not been agnostics but have been converts to a non-Christian and anti-Christian religion. This anti-Christian religion has taken various forms: Communism or Fascism or, in the democratic part of the Western World, Nationalism. But all these have been some form of the worship of the collective power of Man in place of the worship of God. And this man-worship has given birth, as we know, to a practice that is horrifying to everyone who follows the Christian code of conduct, whether he is still a professing Christian or whether he has become a liberal ex-Christian. So, in the Russian and Italian and German provinces of Christendom in our time, the picture has differed from the picture that we get from looking at the Abkhazian and Calabrian and Scandinavian provinces. In Russia and Italy and Germany in our time, we have seen the profession of Christian beliefs and the practice of Christian virtues varying, not inversely with one another, but concomitantly.

But here again we at once find ourselves confronted with the difficulty of striking a spiritual average. When we say that the standard of Christian conduct has varied concomitantly with the abandonment of the profession of Christianity in those countries, we are thinking, of course, of the atrocities that have been committed by the totalitarian governments while in power there. But those atrocities have been initiated by a neo-pagan minority that has seized power by force; and we are led to ask ourselves: How far has the majority of the people in each of these countries been implicated in the responsibility for the atrocities? Clearly it is implicated, and implicated very considerably, first because it has allowed the atrocious minority to come into power, and then because it has not overthrown the minority after having seen that it is atrocious, and finally because many of the ordinary people of those countries have put themselves, or anyway have passively allowed themselves to be put, at the disposal of the atrocious minority for carrying out its orders. So undoubtedly, in those countries governed by a neo-pagan minority, the majority does bear a very considerable share of the responsibility. And yet the actual amount is peculiarly difficult to assess. When we turn from looking at the mote in their eye to the beam in our own eye, and ask ourselves how far we are responsible for the acts of our own less atrocious and less totalitarian governments—acts which we may deprecate but which we have not effectively opposed—we see the difficulty of passing judgement on the majority of ordinary people like ourselves in the totalitarian countries.

Furthermore, in those countries the atrocious neo-pagan minority in power has not been the only minority. In each of them all the time, under the utmost pressure, there has still always been a minority of professing Christians and of liberal ex-Christians who have resisted the neo-pagan minority in power in defence of Christian principles of conduct. And this resisting minority in the totalitarian countries has risked and sacrificed more than has been required of contemporary Christians and liberal ex-Christians in democratic countries. In contemporary Russia and Italy and Germany there have been Christian, agnostic, and atheist martyrs to Christian principles of conduct. In a country where the rulers are neo-pagans who have been countenanced, and even in some cases aided and abetted, by ordinary people, but have been resisted by a handful of martyrs who have given their lives, in some cases, in resisting evil, how are we to strike a spiritual average? Here again the spiritual gamut seems to be very wide.

There is another disconcerting point about the totalitarian ideologies which brings me on to highly controversial ground. These ideologies are *neo*-pagan and *ex*-Christian; they are not primitive pagan and pre-Christian, and they carry in them the traces of their Christian and Jewish past. For instance, their myths are inspired by the myths of Christianity and Judaism. When I use the word "myth," of course I do not mean fairy stories or things that are not true. I am using the word "myth" in the sense in which Plato uses it, and, after all, it is a Greek word, so a Greek philosopher has the right to assign it its meaning; and Plato means by "myth" a form of expression to which one turns when the resources of the intellect have been exhausted and yet one still has something of immense importance and significance which one must express somehow. Communism has taken over from Judaism the myth of the Chosen People; the myth of the miraculous victory of the Chosen People over the heathen who rage furiously together against them; and the myth of the earthly paradise after the victory of Zion has been achieved. These are all Jewish and Christian images of the reality of spiritual life. They have all been adopted by Communism and have influenced its spirit. And then, as we look at the conduct of the totalitarian neo-pagan faiths, we shall find, I fear, that their conduct has been inspired by one vein in the Christian and Jewish tradition of conduct—I mean, the vein of fanaticism and intolerance which one can see if one looks back on the history of all the Judaic religions: Islam, Christianity, and Judaism itself. It is a spirit which does not hesitate to try to inculcate its doctrine and practice by persecution —a spirit that, in all these three religions, is very shocking to people brought up on Hinduism or Buddhism or some other faith of Hindu origin when they look at the conduct of the western half of the World. This vein of fanaticism was not a feature of the primitive, pre-Christian form of paganism. If one reads the *procès verbaux* of the trials of the Christian martyrs—and a number of authentic records have survived—one finds that in many cases the Roman magistrate was eager not to be compelled to pass the death sentence, and that it was the Christian martyr who deliberately left the magistrate no alternative except to pass it. Now I do not believe that, if one could have an authentic record of the trials that have taken place in our lifetime in totalitarian countries, one would find the magistrate informed by that humanitarian spirit. I think he would turn out to have been informed by a much more fanatical spirit, and I think one could trace that fanatical spirit back to the Christian and Jewish past of those totalitarian countries. I think it has been inherited by post-Christian neo-paganism from Christianity and Judaism, and I think its ultimate inspiration is one of two Christian and Jewish conceptions of God which, as I see it, are incompatible with one another.

Christianity and Judaism have one vision of God as being self-sacrificing love—God the merciful, the compassionate, according to the Islamic formula—and another vision of God as being a jealous God. I know that this is a very controversial subject, and I think some psychologists, and many theologians, would contend that the two concepts, though they may seem incompatible, are in truth, inseparable from each other. But these two visions of the nature of God seem to me, at any rate, to be irreconcilable, and the presence of both visions side by side in the common tradition of Christianity and Judaism and Islam has produced in these three Judaic religions an inner contradiction, which, I should say, has never been resolved. One can also see, I think, that this duality of vision is reflected in a duality of conduct. The jealous god's chosen people easily fall into becoming intolerant persecutors. The worshippers of the god who is love—God the merciful, the compassionate—try to act on the belief that their fellow creatures are their brothers, because they are all God's children. These two conflicting elements in the Judaic religions will keep on confronting us in these pages.

If we have come to the conclusion that neither beliefs nor practice offer any clear criteria for making comparisons between religions, we might have to admit that we have drawn blank. But is there not a third element in religion which underlies and inspires both practice and beliefs? (I am thinking of practice in the sense, not just of rites, but of the conduct of life, and I am thinking of beliefs in the intuitive sense as well as in the formal theological sense.) What I have in mind here is something that one might call the attitude or the spirit of a religion. I will try to illustrate what I mean by examples taken from the group of religions that I have called "the higher religions."

First of all, in their attitude toward Man, the higher religions all agree, I believe, in feeling, and feeling intensely, that Man is not the spiritually highest presence known to Man. When it comes to trying to see and describe, and even more when it comes to trying to define, what that higher spiritual presence is, you find a great diversity in the positive presentation of it in the higher religions, a diversity ranging from the concept of it as Brahman or as Nirvana to the concept of it as a personal god. But when you look at the previous negative belief which makes possible this variety of positive beliefs— the negative belief that Man himself is not the spiritually highest presence known to Man—you find, I think, an identity of feeling among all the higher religions. Of course, an identical attitude does not provide a criterion for comparing these religions with one another. But it does provide a criterion for comparing the higher religions, as a group, with each of the two varieties of primitive lower religions; on the one hand, with the worship of Nature and, on the other hand, with the worship of Man in the form of Man's collective power.

Nature-worship agrees, I think, on this negative but crucial point, with the higher religions as against man-worship. For man-worship, Man is the highest presence in the Universe. For nature-worship, as for the higher religions, Man finds himself in the presence of powers much greater than he is which are a mystery to him. Perhaps the two visions of God, which I have called irreconcilable in the Judaic group of higher religions, have their roots in nature-worship and in man-worship respectively. It looks, from the historian's angle of vision, as if the vision of God as being self-sacrificing love has, at any rate, one of its roots in the previous worship of a vegetation-god who dies to give Man sustenance. In the vegetation religion, the god dies to give Man the material bread of life—the physical image on which the higher concept of the spiritual bread of life is based. The vision of God as being a jealous god undoubtedly has at least one of its roots in the worship of the tribe in the form of the god of the Chosen People, representing their collective power.

Next let us consider the attitude toward evil. I think that, here again, there are two points in which all religions agree. The first point is that they all feel that Man ought to take sides with good against evil. This pair of

opposite terms, good and evil, carries in itself the idea
of an obligation to take sides against what is evil and
in support of what is good. That is one point, I think, on
which all religions agree. A second point is that Man
must try to place himself in harmony with that spiritual
presence in the Universe that is spiritually greater than
Man—a presence that, in personal terms, reveals itself
as god, and, in its impersonal facet, as absolute reality.
The co-existence of those two feelings raises the question
of the relation of God to good and evil; and at this point
I apologize, as a non-theologian, for treading on what is
rather well-worn theological ground, on which the last
word has been said, perhaps, long ago. I apologize, but I
shall not hold back, for this is a problem which we can
never evade; we must keep on returning to it and trying
to find our way through it, though Man has not solved
it yet. The elements of the problem are very obvious.
If God is the author of evil as well as good, as He must
be if He is absolute and all-inclusive, Man will be embracing evil as well as good in putting himself in harmony
with God. But to embrace evil is by definition wrong.
On the other hand, if, in putting himself in harmony
with God, Man is embracing good only, as is right, then
God cannot be absolute all-inclusive reality. He can be
only a part or fragment of absolute reality, like Man. But
that is by definition untrue. And in this dilemma Man
has, and always has had, to choose between saving truth
and saving goodness. I am not thinking of a conscious in-

tellectual choice, because, long before this choice was formulated in the intellectual terms of philosophy and theology, the great religions had, each of them, made their own choices intuitively. And here, I think, one finds a difference of attitude that provides a criterion for comparing them.

Hinduism, if I have read it right, intuitively seeks to save the absoluteness of God at the cost of His goodness. The Judaic religions intuitively try to save His goodness at the cost of His absoluteness. And neither solution has been a true solution, because, for human beings, God has to be *both* absolute *and* good, and the two requirements cannot be reconciled in terms of logic, though perhaps they may be reconcilable in terms of the myths to which Plato resorts when reason fails him. God's goodness cannot be vindicated fully except at the price of dualism, and the religions of the Judaic group do not go to that length in their sacrifice of God's absoluteness. They do not attribute evil to God directly, but they do attribute evil to the Devil, and they do not make the Devil an independent god. He is one of God's creatures, though a rebellious one, and this leaves God, who is the Devil's creator, still indirectly responsible for the Devil and for the evil that the Devil does. This is the reason why, throughout the history of Christianity, there have been repeated deviations from the main stream of the Christian tradition in the direction of dualism. These have been attempts to save God's goodness completely at the sacri-

fice of His absoluteness. I am thinking of Marcionism
in the second century; I am thinking of early medieval
Paulicianism and Bogomilism in the Eastern Orthodox
Christian World, and of Catharism in Western Christendom. I am also thinking of our own modern Western
poet Blake in recent times. It is no accident, I think, that
there has been this recurrence of outbursts of dualism
in the history of Christianity. Conversely, Hinduism, in
vindicating God's absoluteness, does not go to the length
of denying the moral difference between good and evil;
and for Hindus, this leaves an unresolved conflict between Man's obligation to put himself in harmony with
God in all His aspects and Man's obligation to take the
side of what is good against what is evil. To the Christian,
the Hindu attitude toward the problem of evil may seem
rather shocking. How can you worship a god who is evil
as well as good? On the other hand, the Hindu is left in-
tellectually unsatisfied by the Christian-Jewish-Muslim
attitude towards the same problem. How can you believe
in an absolute reality that does not include evil as well as
good?

Lastly, we have to consider the attitude towards the
problem of suffering. The attitude towards suffering is
an attitude that underlies theological beliefs. It also
underlies, and perhaps eventually determines, conduct
and practice. It is a datum of experience that suffering
is a product of desire; that, by extinguishing desire, we
can extinguish suffering, too; and that suffering cannot

be extinguished totally by any means short of extinguishing all desire. These Buddhist axioms, which provide the starting-point for Buddhist ascetic practice, would, I think, be accepted by everybody as being statements of matters of fact. But, when confronted with the necessity of choosing a policy towards suffering, Christianity and the older school of Buddhism, the so-called Hinayana school, intuitively take different lines; and they take their different lines, I believe, because they have different ideas about what is the highest good, about what is the true end of Man.

The older school of Buddhism assumes that the true end of Man, and the paramount objective of human spiritual endeavors, is to extinguish suffering; and therefore, as a means towards this end, it sets itself to extinguish desire, without discriminating between different kinds of desire. It sets itself to extinguish all desire, because it has correctly diagnosed that suffering is inseparable from desire, and, short of extinguishing all desire, you cannot extinguish all suffering. Christianity, I think, begins by assuming that there is a distinction, and one of vital importance, between two different kinds of desire. In the Christian view there are self-centered desires which are bad, and which should therefore be extinguished by Christians as resolutely and ruthlessly as a Buddhist would attempt to extinguish all desires. But the Christian would draw a distinction between those self-centered desires and desires of another kind—self-devoting or self-sacrificing desires—which are good, and which should therefore be acted upon, however great may be the cost of this in terms of suffering. For Christianity, the true end of Man, and the paramount objective of human endeavors, is not to extinguish suffering, but to follow the lead of Man's good desires—in fact, to follow the lead of love, even if love leads to the Cross. As Christianity sees it, to incur suffering is a lesser evil than to extinguish love; and I would say more than that. I would say that, in the Christian view, if the Christian who suffers for love can rise to the occasion, his suffering may not be just a lesser evil; it may become a positive good, because, in suffering for love, he would be putting himself in harmony with the God who is love and who has shown what He is by what He has done: by His incarnation and His crucifixion. By following God's example, the Christian may be helping to awake a responsive love in other souls.

This Christian glorification of suffering in the cause of love can be very shocking to non-Christians. I once heard the following story told of an English family living in China who engaged a Chinese nurse for their small children. As soon as this Chinese woman came into their house, they saw that she was much disturbed by something, and, as the hours and days passed, she showed signs of being more and more upset. Naturally, they were anxious to discover the reason, but she was very shy of telling them. At last, with great embarrassment, she said:

"Well, there is something that I just cannot understand. You are obviously good people; you obviously love your children and care for them; yet, in every room in this house and even on the staircase as well, I see repeated reproductions of a picture of a criminal being put to death by some horrible form of torture which we have never heard of in China; and I cannot understand how you—responsible people and loving parents as you obviously are—I cannot understand how you can expose your children to the dreadful effects of seeing this awful picture, at every turn, at this early impressionable stage of their lives." The interesting point about this story is that the simple-minded and naïve comment of the Chinese nurse, with her Confucian and Buddhist background, on those pictures of the Crucifixion would also have been the comment of a sophisticated pre-Christian Greek or Roman Stoic or Epicurean philosopher. Like the Buddhists of the older school, the Stoics and the Epicureans made it their aim to cast out all feelings, including feelings of pity and love, in order to detach themselves from desire.

From the Christian point of view, it is interesting to observe that, as we look at the record of the Buddha's life, one of the most sublime things in it, as Christians see it, is that the Buddha did not practice what He preached. You know the story of His temptation at the moment after His enlightenment. The tempter said to Him: "Now that you have attained enlightenment, you can step straight out of This World into Nirvana and enter into your perpetual rest." But the Buddha refused. He elected to remain in the World for the term of His natural life in order to help other people to find the path which He himself had trodden to the point where there was only the one final step still to take. In a sense this was inconsequent; for, if it was right to exhort other people to kill desire in order to extricate themselves from suffering, it must have been logically right for the Buddha Himself to extricate Himself by taking that final step into Nirvana at the earliest opportunity. He was illogical in feeling and acting on a compassion for all other sentient beings, and this illogicality that comes out in the difference between His practice and His preaching will strike a Christian as being akin to the Christian attitude. So perhaps the attitude towards suffering, even more than the attitude towards evil, does provide a criterion for comparing different higher religions with one another.

I have now suggested to you some possible criteria, and have tried to apply them as means of assessing the several higher religions' weaker and stronger points. We shall have to consider the attitude towards evil and the attitude towards suffering again in the last chapter, when we shall be discussing the question: What should be the Christian approach to the living non-Christian faiths?

II

What Are the Characteristics of the Contemporary World?

II

IN this second chapter I want to say something about the characteristics of the contemporary world, because this is the world in which Christianity and the other living faiths all find themselves living today. We are conscious, all of us, in our day that the world is in process of going through a revolution. Under our eyes in our lifetime we are seeing an old world dissolving and a new world coming into existence; and this great secular revolution, through which we feel ourselves to be passing, seems likely to produce a revolution in the relations between the religions.

Let me remind you of one or two of the features of that old world that is now passing away. One of them, which is paradoxical from the point of view of religion, is that, in this old world, and the old world is still partly with us today, "a meridian decides what is the truth." When Pascal coined that famous phrase—when he said that what is truth on this side of the Pyrenees is error on the other side of the Pyrenees—he was speaking, not about religion, but about law. But in the map of the old world Pascal's dictum does apply to religion as well.

One can take a map of the face of this planet and plot out on it the present geographical distribution of the higher religions. One can pin-point their holy places and their pilgrimage-resorts in each case; and, if one does that, one finds that they fall into two clearly defined geographical groups. One of these two groups is centered on a holy land in India—the middle part of the Ganges Valley in the province of Bihar—which contains both the chief holy place of Buddhism at Bodh Gaya, where the Buddha received His enlightenment, and the chief holy place of Hinduism at Benares. And then there is a, to us, more familiar second holy land in Southwest Asia, in Palestine and in the adjoining part of Arabia called the Hijaz—a holy land which contains Jerusalem, the chief holy place of Judaism and Christianity and the third holy place of Islam, and which also contains Mecca and Medina, which are the first and second holy places of Islam. Round each of those two centers the religions of the Indian group and the religions of the Southwest-Asian group have come, by our time, to be distributed in two concentric circles; and in both groups the youngest member of the group occupies today the cradle of this group of religions at its circle's center.

In the Southwest-Asian group, which you might also call the Hijazi-Palestinian group, Islam today occupies the center, and Islam's older sister Christianity has been pushed out in four different directions. Nestorian Christianity has been pushed out eastwards into Kurdistan

and Southern India, Monophysite Christianity southwards into Abyssinia, Orthodox Christianity northwards
into Russia, and Catholic and Protestant ex-Catholic
Christianity westwards, first into Western Europe and
then across the Atlantic into the Americas. Judaism,
which is the oldest religion in the group and is the mother
of both Christianity and Islam has, for the most part,
been ground to pieces into a "diaspora," a "dispersion
among the gentiles." Judaism has not retained possession
of definite territories of its own except here and there
where it has been lodged in mountain fastness near the
outer edges of the circle. If you look at the religious map
of the Caucasus, you will find in some of the most inaccessible mountains of the Caucasus some outlying Jewish populations, and if you look at the religious map of
Abyssinia on the extreme southern rim of the circle cen-
tering on Palestine, you will find, here again, adherents
of Judaism in some of the most inaccessible mountains
of Abyssinia. Round these Abyssinian Jews you will find
an inner ring of Monophysite Christians and an outer
ring of Muslims.

In the Indian group, Hinduism today occupies the
center; and Hinduism's—modern Hinduism's—contemporary and sister, the younger or Mahayanian ("greater
vehicle") school of Buddhism, has been pushed out northwards. It was originally pushed out into Afghanistan and
Central Asia; and, although Buddhism is extinct in those
countries today, its passage through them is attested by

the imposing religious monuments that it has left behind it there, especially in Afghanistan. From Central Asia the northern school of Buddhism has travelled on to become an ubiquitous faith, but nowhere the exclusive faith, in Eastern Asia—in China above all, but also in the lesser East-Asian countries: Korea, Japan, and Vietnam. The older, so-called Hinayanian ("lesser vehicle") school of Buddhism, which is the oldest religion surviving in this Indian group and is the mother, I should say, not only of the northern school of Buddhism but also of the post-Buddhaic form of Hinduism too, has been pushed by Hinduism out of India into Ceylon and from Ceylon it has evangelized Southeastern Asia: Burma, Siam (Thailand), and Cambodia.

You will observe that the original map of the distribution of the two groups of higher religions was remarkably symmetrical. You find these two circles, and find the religions radiating out concentrically, one after the other, from each of the two centers. But that rather neat and tidy map has been distorted during the last four or five centuries by the temporary world-wide ascendancy of the Protestant and Catholic Christianity of Western Europe, reinforced latterly by the overseas extension of Western Europe in the Americas. This ascendancy is passing away within our lifetime; but at the same time it is leaving effects upon the World that seem likely to outlast it; and one of the most important of them has been its effect on the world-map of the religions. West-

ern Europe's commercial, military, political, and economic expansion overseas has carried Western Christianity to all the coasts of the World, and from the
coasts, in the course of several centuries, it has gradually
been penetrating into the interior of the continents. It
has been spread partly through the conversion of pre-
Columbian populations, and partly through the supplant-
ing of pre-Columbian populations by settlers of Western
European origin. The most conspicuous examples of both
these processes are to be found in the Americas. Middle
America and the Andean countries of South America
have been won for Western Christianity mainly through
the forcible conversion of the pre-Columbian populations. North America, north of the Rio Grande, and,
in South America, Brazil, Uruguay, Argentina, and Chile,
have been won for Western Christianity mainly
through colonization from Western Europe.

The temporary ascendancy of the West Europeans
and their colonists has now also brought about a revolutionary change in the distribution of Judaism, because
the Jewish dispersion in Western Europe and the Americas, particularly in the United States, has shared in the
power of the non-Jewish majority of the Western Society, and this power, this Western power, has enabled
the Jews to reconquer a foothold in Palestine in our own
lifetime. They have not managed to recover the original
territories of Judah and Israel, but they have conquered
what used to be the territory of the Philistines between

the hill country of Judah and Israel and the shores of the Mediterranean.

So it is not only possible to plot out a map of the present distribution of the higher religions; it is also possible to trace this distribution to its historical causes; and the strange thing is that most of these causes are non-religious; they derive from physical geography or from technology or from politics or war or economics, not from religion. This is paradoxical, because neither the professions nor the practice of any of the higher religions seem to have any intrinsic connection with historical geography. Insofar as the likenesses and differences between these religions can be accounted for by any natural phenomena, the phenomena that count are evidently not geographical but spiritual or psychological; and the illuminating diagram, one would expect, would be, not a chart of the globe, but a chart of the soul, what in the language of the Indian religions is called a *mandala*.

One could also draw a map of the former geographical distribution of the older, what one might call the lower, religions, which the higher religions have now largely replaced; and it would not be paradoxical to find that we could express the lower religions in terms of geography, because all those lower religions were, I think, forms either of nature-worship or of man-worship; and both those species of religion are, by their very nature, confined within geographical limits. It is true that there are some objects of nature-worship—I am thinking of the

Sun, the Moon, the Planets, the Sky, the Sea—which are world-wide; and the worship of these world-wide natural objects has, as we know, prepared the way for the advent of the higher religions. But most natural objects are local. Even the fixed stars in the firmament are different for inhabitants of the Northern and inhabitants of the Southern Hemisphere.

And then think of the cultivated plants which have played so great a part as objects of worship in the worship of Nature and which have entered so deeply into the imagery and the emotions of the higher religions that have supplanted nature-worship. When an inhabitant of the Western half of the Old World mentions the word "wheat" or the word "wine," he imagines that he is speaking of something that is world-wide. But so does the inhabitant of the eastern half of the Old World when he mentions the word "rice"; he too imagines that he is speaking of something that is world-wide. In reality, even these most widely distributed of all the fruits of the Earth are none of them world-wide—neither wheat, nor rice, nor the vine, nor the olive. I can remember the startling effect on me of visiting Japan, when I walked out into the country and tried to ask for bread and found that there was no word for bread in the Japanese language. By nature there is no such thing as bread in Japan, and the Japanese use a Portuguese word, "pan," to describe this, for them, exotic staff of life. There is no wine either in Japan. Any fermented drink that is drunk there

is made from rice and not from grapes. It gave me a
curious feeling to discover that the symbols of the Christian religion, which seem so universal to Westerners, are
in a sense parochial. A meridian decides the symbols.
On this side of the line they are bread and wine; on the
other side, they will be rice and, let us say, cocoanut milk.

There are other objects of nature-worship—rivers,
mountains, stones, and trees—that have a still narrower
geographical range than such crops as wheat and rice.
It is true that people come a long way to visit a sacred
stone. Think of how far the pilgrims come every year
to do reverence to the sacred stone that is built into the
Ka'bah at Mecca. Still, on the whole, rivers, mountains,
stones, and trees, being by nature local, have a relatively
narrow geographical radius as objects of worship; and
the objects of man-worship are also local where Man is
worshipped in the form of collective human power. Collective human power is mainly embodied in states and
their rulers, and, during the last few thousand years, the
rulers of states and the states themselves have been, I
suppose, by far the commonest objects of worship,
avowed or unavowed, of the great majority of the human
race. Yet the largest of these states that have been objects of worship or idols, the largest of them known to
history so far, have covered only small fractions of the
total land surface of our globe.

The Roman Empire and the Chinese Empire, each of
which was deified in its own way, were each regarded by

its inhabitants and worshippers as being co-extensive with the *oikoumenê*, the whole of the inhabited land surface of the globe. Yet those two deified empires co-existed on the surface of the globe for several centuries without coming into direct contact with one another. There was an indirect trade between them in a few luxury goods; and there is a record, in the Chinese official history of the Han dynasty, of one embassy from the Roman Emperor Marcus Aurelius which arrived at Canton; but, if these two self-styled "world empires" did just brush against one another with the tips of their antennae, the contact was very slight. Today the United States and the Soviet Union, like the ancient Roman Empire and the ancient Chinese Empire, seem large when measured by the average size of a present-day European state; and they seem very large indeed if we include in each of them their respective allies and satellites. Yet the fact that these two huge power blocks, in their turn, co-exist in the World today shows how far both of them are from being world-wide. So geography is intrinsically relevant to the objects of worship of the lower religions, whether those objects of worship are forces or phenomena of Nature or whether they are groupings of collective human power.

All higher religions agree with one another in repudiating both man-worship and nature-worship. But the followers of some of the higher religions have accused and do accuse the followers of others of playing false to their common profession of this extremely important negative tenet of repudiating both forms of lower religion. For example, in Christian and Muslim eyes, Hinduism seems to stand convicted of having failed to break with nature-worship. I imagine that, in face of that charge, a philosophic-minded Hindu would probably make the same reply that in the eighteenth century a Neapolitan Roman Catholic saint would have made to a contemporary Protestant critic of the contemporary spiritual condition of the Neapolitan peasantry. My hypothetical Hindu, like my imaginary eighteenth-century Neapolitan Christian saint, would say that the lower forms of nature-worship had been deliberately spared and left intact because they are a necessary avenue for the unsophisticated mass of mankind; and the great mass of mankind is still very ignorant and unsophisticated. They are, my Hindu would say, a necessary avenue for them if they are to make an approach to the esoteric doctrine which is the true Hindu faith. He would say that it is better to have your foot on the lowest rung of the ladder than not to have it on any rung at all; and he would go on to say that, if your foot is set on the lowest rung, you may perhaps gradually climb the ladder to one of the higher rungs.

Then again, a monotheistic-minded Jew or Muslim would accuse Christianity of having diluted monotheism with man-worship. As you know, when a Muslim wishes to speak rudely about Christians, he calls them "polytheists." A Christian would reply that, in worshipping Christ Jesus, he is worshipping God; but the Jew and the Muslim would probably retort that Christianity was aggravating its impiety by identifying a man with the one true God instead of admitting frankly that it had relapsed into man-worship and polytheism.

In these unhappy controversies between the higher religions, Hinduism and Christianity may be in the right against their critics, but their apologists may not have made the right defence. It might be a better reply to admit the charges on the line that I have attributed to my imaginary Hindu philosopher, and to plead that God has revealed Himself to some extent in each religion, lower as well as higher, and that, if that is true, the right attitude for the followers of all the higher religions toward the lower religions would be, not to try to eradicate them root and branch, but to try to incorporate any elements in them that could be made to serve the higher religions' spiritual purposes. If a Muslim accuses a Christian of having incorporated elements from the worship of Nature or the worship of Man, the Christian could retort to the Muslim that the prophet Muhammad himself deliberately incorporated into Islam some of the salient elements in the pre-Islamic paganism of Western Arabia—for example, the pilgrimage to Mecca and the veneration of the Black Stone. The Muslim, so the Christian might maintain, ought to remind himself of that fact before he attacks either the Christian

or the Hindu for falling away from the straight path
of the rejection of nature-worship and man-worship.

Again, all the higher religions agree with one another
in rejecting and condemning the rite of human sacrifice
as practiced, for example, in the past by the Canaanites
and by the Aztecs—a rite practiced as a means of appeas-
ing and fortifying the gods of Nature. Cortés and his
fellow Spanish conquerors of Mexico were very brutal
men; yet you cannot read the narratives of their ex-
periences that have been recorded by Cortés himself
and by one or two of his companions without realizing
that they were genuinely shocked and horrified by the
Middle American practice of human sacrifice. It was
just an accident, I suppose, that Mexico was discovered
and conquered by Castilian Christians and not by Otto-
man Muslims. It was rather touch and go, which of those
two Mediterranean seafaring peoples would be the first
to reach the New World. But I am sure that, if the
brigand from the Old World who conquered Mexico
had been a Muslim Turkish corsair instead of a Christian
Spanish corsair, Khayr-ed-Din would have been just
as much shocked as Cortés was by the rite of human sacrifice that he would have found, as Cortés found it, pre-
vailing in Mexico.

All the same, this rite of human sacrifice is very deeply
imbedded in the past of some of the higher religions.
The Canaanite rite of sacrificing one's eldest son was
practiced in Judah down to the seventh century before

the beginning of the Christian Era; and, in the Greater
Canaan overseas in Northwest Africa, human sacrifice
was not suppressed until after the beginning of the
Christian Era. In recent years we have recovered some
of the remains of one of the northernmost of the Phoeni-
cian cities along the coast of Syria, at the site now called
Ras ash-Shamrah, and in ancient times Ugarit. Among
the discoveries have been tablets inscribed in an alphabet
selected from the cuneiform characters; and some of these
tablets record fragments of Canaanite mythology. In
those fragmentary records of Canaanite mythology, we
find the rite of sacrifice being projected from the world
of men into the world of gods. We find the god Mot,
the god of vegetation, being sacrificed by the goddess
Anat, and we find another god, the son of Danel, the son
of El, being sacrificed too.

To Jews and Christians and Muslims, this rite of
human sacrifice seems abominable, and its translation,
in this Canaanite mythology, from Earth to Heaven
seems to them impious. Yet this abominable rite has
been, I think, one of the sources of inspiration of the
sublime and profound Christian vision of a God the Son
who voluntarily sacrifices Himself for the salvation of
His creatures. Moreover, the Aztec and Canaanite rite
of human sacrifice, which is so detestable in our eyes, was
right and obligatory for its practitioners in their eyes. It
was felt by Abraham, according to the story told in the
Old Testament, to be obligatory upon him until he was

released at the last moment by the substitution of a ram for Isaac. This notion of a vicarious sacrifice, of the substitution of one victim for another, is familiar to us in the Christian imagery of the vicarious sacrifice of a lamb; and in recent years our Western archeologists who have been excavating the site of the ancient Canaanite colonial city of Carthage and digging up the grim *tophet*, the place where human sacrifice—above all, the sacrifice of infant human beings—was carried out, have come across the record of *molk amor*. The earlier layer of the remains of sacrificial victims seems to consist of the remains of human children. But in the later layers there are jars, containing the remains of the sacrifice, which are marked with two words that have been interpreted, though I believe the interpretation is contentious, to mean "sacrifice of a lamb." It has been supposed that in Carthage, as in the homeland, Canaan itself, the animal was gradually substituted for the human being as the sacrificial victim.

This strange story of human sacrifice, and of its intertwining with the higher religions, brings out two points. One is that comparative value judgements are subjective. When we judge between ourselves and Mesha king of Moab, who saved his country by sacrificing his eldest son, or between ourselves and Agamemnon, who won a fair wind for the Achaean armada by sacrificing his daughter Iphigeneia, we find ourselves inevitably passing judgement on them both. But we should remind ourselves, as we pass it, that we judge between them and ourselves at our peril. The second point is that human beings cannot avoid making comparative value judgements, even though this involves them, as it does involve them, in playing the part of judges in a case in which they are also parties. The fact that we are also parties should lead us to feel humility and to exercise caution and restraint in making our judgements, and not to suppose that our judgements are complete or all-wise or, above all, final.

Up to this point in this chapter I have been talking about the old world that is now passing away before our eyes. Today, I think, we can see the World changing from one in which a man's religion used to be decided for him a priori by his birthplace, by the accident of birth, into a world in which, to a greater and greater degree, as the World grows together, he will be able to make a free choice, as an adult, between alternative religions. This change is being produced by a number of factors—first and foremost, by the world-wide expansion of the modern Western civilization within these last four or five hundred years. The West has been captivating and unifying the World partly by military conquest, partly by economic penetration, partly by what we call in a simile "the annihilation of distance" through the achievements of our modern Western technology, and partly, and perhaps most fruitfully and significantly, by the voluntary conversion of non-Westerners to the

Western way of life. The cumulative effect of all these processes, operating over the course of several centuries, is by now very great.

Here is another point that I should like to put before you. This Western civilization that is now unifying the World in these various ways is a post-Christian or ex-Christian civilization. Of course, it has not made, and cannot make, an absolute break with its past. It is difficult to divest oneself of one's past. If you look at the history of Russia since 1917, and look into it critically, you will see how very hard it is to divest oneself of one's past, even when one is making the utmost conscious and deliberate efforts to do so. And so, in our Western World, our late modern secular way of life is still a Christian one in many ways, and many members of the Western society are still consciously trying to lead a Christian life. But the surviving features of the Christian way of life are now, I should say, no longer our civilization's distinctive features. They are not its distinctive features in the eyes of us Westerners ourselves, and, what is a good deal more important, they are not its distinctive features in the eyes of the non-Western majority of the human race into whose life the Western civilization is now radiating out its powerful influence. In their eyes today, the distinctive feature of our Western civilization is obviously its technology. In our eyes I think it is probably the sacredness of the civil rights of the individual. I shall have something to say later about the

relation of that sense of the sacredness of secular individual rights to Christianity and Judaism. But, in the
form in which we now cherish our secular civil rights,
I think our feeling about them is rather remote from
their origins.

This secularization of the Western civilization, which
began towards the close of the seventeenth century, has
had a revolutionary effect on the fortunes of our civilization abroad. In the first chapter of Western expansion,
which ran from the close of the fifteenth century to the
close of the seventeenth, Westerners were still loyal
members of the Christian Church, and they were also
fanatical champions of it in the sense of believing it to be
their duty to impose Christianity by force where they
had the power. In resorting to force for this purpose they
were in the wrong, but they were not in the wrong in
seeking to propagate their civilization in its integral
form, with Western Christianity as the principal element
in it.

However, in this integral, would-be Western Christian,
form the Western civilization was rejected in the seventeenth century by the rest of the World. The story
of its rejection in Japan is familiar to us. You know
that the Japanese sent a commission to Western Europe
to study Christianity in the early years of the seventeenth
century. The commission made an unfavorable report
on its return, and in the end Christianity was banned
and the Christian missionaries, and, with them, the lay

Portuguese traders, were banished from Japan and were forbidden to return. As you also know, the same thing happened in China towards the end of the seventeenth century and in the early years of the eighteenth century. Perhaps we are less generally aware that, in the sixteen-thirties, the very years in which Christianity was being banned in Japan by the non-Christian authorities there, Western Christianity was being expelled from Abyssinia by the local Monophysite Christians, and this for the same reason. There was a domineering attitude on the part of the Western Christians in propagating their religion that caused a revolt, not only among non-Christians, but among Christians of non-Western varieties of Christianity. There was the same struggle in Southern India between the Roman Catholic missionaries of Western Christianity there in the sixteenth and seventeenth centuries and the local South Indian Church. This church was originally Nestorian, but in the early years of the seventeenth century it joined the Monophysite Church in order to obtain stronger backing for resisting the attempts of the Roman Catholic Western missionaries to bring the South Indian Christians into the Western Christian fold. The only permanent conquests made in the early modern age of Western expansion by the Western civilization in its integral Christian form were among the pre-Columbian populations of Middle America and of the Andean part of South America; and those populations were literally conquered by superior military force and more potent military technique.

By contrast, the second chapter of our modern Western expansion, which began towards the close of the
seventeenth century, has been brilliantly successful.
Within these last two hundred and fifty years the whole
World has been penetrated by our Western civilization;
and this time the reception of our civilization has been
voluntary to a very considerable extent. The Chinese and
Japanese have, each of them, reversed their former
policy of exclusion. They have reopened themselves to
Western influence and have deliberately embraced our
Western civilization. But the latter-day Western civilization that has won these great successes has not been
an integral Western civilization. It has been an extract
from the Christian Western civilization—an extract
from which the Christianity has been deliberately and
almost ostentatiously left out. Of course, I am not for-
getting the mighty works of Catholic and Protestant
Western missionaries in the later as well as in the earlier
modern age of Western expansion. Those missionaries
have sown the seeds of non-Western branches of the
Catholic Church and of the several Protestant Churches
in all the continents. But these late modern Western
missionaries of Christianity have not played the domi-
nant and decisive part in the late modern expansion of
the Western civilization that their predecessors played
in the early modern age of Western expansion in the
sixteenth and seventeenth centuries. In this later period
of expansion, Western businessmen and Western colonial
administrators have had the upper hand over the West-

ern missionaries. These businessmen and administrators have not been unmindful of the earlier chapter in the history of Western expansion and of the connection between the rather high-handed attempt to spread Western Christianity in the Portuguese and Spanish age of expansion and the rejection of the Western civilization when it was propagated in that form. So they have been on the watch, during these last two centuries, to see to it that the missionaries shall not be allowed to prejudice what the laymen have considered to be the West's commercial and political interests.

It is true that in late modern Western colonial administration, for instance in tropical Africa in the field of education, the governments have to some extent changed their attitude towards the missionaries and have sought their co-operation in this field at any rate. But, on the whole, the attitude of the governments towards the missionaries has been watchful and suspicious, and they have taken pains to show the people whom they have been ruling in Asia and Africa, or the people with whom they have been trading, that, while they are determined to rule them, and determined to trade with them, they are not going to make that an excuse for trying to convert them from their ancestral religion to the ancestral religion of the West. So, in this later chapter, the conquests made by Western Christianity have been modest compared with the conquests made by the secular elements in our late modern Western civilization. When

I talk of the secular elements, I am thinking, first and foremost, of Western technology. The whole World is eager to tap this Western cornucopia. But, if you study the attempt of the non-Western societies to come to school in the polytechnical institutes of the West since the close of the seventeenth century, starting with the classic pioneer attempt of Peter the Great in Russia, you will find that all of them alike have aimed at receiving from the West the maximum amount of Western technology while taking the minimum amount of the rest of our Western civilization.

Possibly experience has already shown that this attempt to pick and choose may not be practicable in the long run. If you once commit yourself to taking one element from some alien civilization, you may find yourself led on, in unexpected ways, into being constrained also to receive other elements which, at first sight, might seem to have no connection with the element that you have originally taken intentionally and deliberately. In the long run it may not be possible to take part and leave the rest; but that is what all the non-Western civilizations have been trying to do during the last two hundred years. They have been trying to take as much as possible of our technology and as little as possible of the rest of our civilization.

There is perhaps one exception to that. They have also voluntarily embraced the Western ideal of emancipation. In late modern times the West has placed great value on emancipation—emancipation for Western people themselves in their own home territory—and the rest of the World, the non-Western part of the World, has adopted this ideal from the West. But its main motive in adopting it has perhaps been a wish to use it as an ideological instrument for liberating itself from Western domination; and the word "emancipation" itself, and the idea expressed in the word, turn out to be ambiguous, when we look into them.

There is emancipation in the sense of the ideal of Western liberalism; and this means emancipation for individual human beings in the name of individual human rights; the emancipation of slaves, the emancipation of women, the emancipation of industrial workers, the emancipation of the subject colonial peoples of Asia and Africa. This belief in the rights of individuals is, I believe, of Christian and Jewish origin. The belief in these secular rights is, I think, derived from a belief in the sacredness of human personalities, and this belief evidently has Christian roots. It descends from the Jewish belief that human souls are precious in the sight of God and from the Christian belief that God has given a practical proof of His love for human souls by what He has done in becoming incarnate and in suffering death on the Cross for the sake of their salvation. So one can truly say, I think, that the Western ideal of emancipation for individuals, though it has been secularized and though many of those who care for it today have lost the memory of its religious origin, is nevertheless truly a legacy from Christianity to a post-Christian secular Western civilization.

There is, however, another kind of emancipation which is not only different from the emancipation of individuals but is at variance with it. Hitler is said once to have proclaimed: "I am making all Germans unfree in order to make Germany free." He was proclaiming the ideal of emancipation, not for individual human souls, but for a human ant-heap or bee-hive, for institutions like nations or states or classes that embody collective human power, the ideal of Communism on the Russian side of the Iron Curtain and of Fascism and Nationalism on the Western side. Collective human power was given the name "Leviathan" by the English philosopher Thomas Hobbes, writing under the influence of the painful effects of the unleashing of fanaticism in the English Civil War, which was a backwash from the Western Wars of Religion; and the worship of Leviathan is certainly not derived from Christianity. It is derived from Christianity's earliest and most formidable adversary, man-worship. The worship of collective human power is, I should say, the same in essence whether the collectivity that is deified is some local community like Athens or Britain or the United States or France, or whether it is a would-be world-wide community like the Roman Empire or the Chinese Empire. Would-be world-wide communities may be worthier objects of worship than local communities in the sense that their intentions may be more beneficent than those of local aggregations of power. But, in essence, the object of worship is the same. So the West, and the rest of the World as well, is faced with the question: In which of these two contending and, in fact, incompatible forms is the World going to embrace this modern Western ideal of emancipation? Is it to be emancipation for Leviathan, for some aggregation of collective human power? Or is it to be emancipation for human beings, for human souls? This is a question which is obviously of vital concern not only to Christianity but to all the living higher religions. And this leads on to the further question: In the Westernizing world of our time, what are the prospects for Christianity and for the other living higher religions?

This further question presents itself because, in the arena in which we find ourselves exposed today, all the higher religions are confronted by a formidable common competitor. The danger that confronts them is not a revival of nature-worship. Long ago the higher religions themselves have, all of them, emptied Nature of her divinity by winning a new vision of divinity as God or as some other form of absolute reality beyond Nature, instead of seeing this presence in the Universe that is higher than Man as being immanent in Nature herself. The Jewish-Christian-Muslim vision of a personal God, the Buddhist vision of Nirvana, the Hindu vision of Brahma, have left no place for nature-worship; and this secularization of Nature, which the higher religions have begun, has been completed in our time by modern Western technology. Technology has given nature-worship its death-blow, by making Nature manifestly Man's slave; for one cannot worship something which one feels that he has mastered. So the danger today is not a revival of nature-worship; the danger is a revival of man-worship in the form of a worship of collective human power. And here modern Western technology, so far from exorcising the danger, has immensely aggravated it. This danger is acute today largely because of the extraordinary achievements of our modern Western technology. Technology has raised our collective human power to a quite unprecedented degree of potency; and, like all human beings, in all time and places, who acquire power suddenly, we are in danger of abusing it. We are in danger of abusing it to suppress individual liberty in favor of totalitarianism, both of the Nationalist and of the Communist kind, and we are perhaps even in danger of abusing it to destroy the human race, and perhaps even all life on this planet, by atomic warfare.

A less dangerous form of man-worship is the worship of individual secular human welfare in the non-religious sense of the word "welfare." I do not mean merely the material sense. The secular welfare that we worship includes spiritual values, but these are spiritual values of a non-religious kind. This is the ideal that, in a famous document, is called "the pursuit of happiness"; and, like the pursuit of power, the pursuit of purely secular and mundane happiness is incompatible with the ideals and precepts of the higher religions. But perhaps, unlike the attainment of secular power, the attainment of secular happiness could be an incidental consequence of pursuing the aims of the higher religions. Perhaps it is impossible to attain secular happiness for the individual by pursuing this secular happiness as an ultimate end in itself; but it is conceivable that secular happiness for the individual may be produced as an incidental by-product if the individual is aiming at something else that is spiritually above it and beyond it. Secular happiness may be a by-product of trying to carry out the spiritual aims that are common to all the higher religions: the effort to take sides with what is good against what is evil, and the effort to attain harmony with absolute reality or God. The fable of Solomon's choice is pertinent here. It is only when we seek something beyond the object immediately in view that this lesser object incidentally comes within our grasp.

III

What Is Christianity's Relation to the Western Civilization That Is Unifying the Contemporary World?

III

IN the preceding chapter I was trying to sketch, in
a summary way, some of the characteristics of the
ex-Christian Western civilization that has been captur-
ing and unifying the World. In this chapter I want to
say something about Christianity's relation to this secular society in which we are living. The first suggestion
that I will make is that the association of Christianity
with our Western civilization is only partial and temporary. What is the date at which we can first observe
our present civilization just beginning to sprout up
among the rubble of the ruins of the Roman Empire in
what had been the Roman Empire's western provinces?
We cannot, I think, see this beginning to happen till
about the year 700 of the Christian Era. And think what
Christianity had done and had experienced in the course
of those seven hundred years during which Christianity
had been present in the World before our Western civilization had been seen or heard of.

First of all, think of Christianity spreading round the
shores of the Mediterranean under the Roman Peace,
among the population of the great cities of the Ancient

Greek world—spreading among the industrial workers
and the smaller businessmen in the Eastern Mediterranean and, further west, in the city of Rome itself. In the
Western World that began to arise about the year A.D.
700, not one of those cities that had been the cradles of
Christianity was included. Of course, the physical site
of Rome was included; this site lay just within the extreme southeastern corner of the nascent Western
World. But seventh-century Rome was not the Rome
of the Roman Empire. There was a moment in the course
of the dissolution of the Graeco-Roman civilization in
Italy in the sixth century of the Christian Era—at the
time of the attempted reconquest of the West by the
Roman imperial government at Constantinople—when
the population of the city of Rome was reduced from its
previous maximum of a million or perhaps a million and
a half to no more than four hundred souls; and, though
Rome became rather more populous again later on, the
catastrophe that she had suffered in the sixth century had
made a very great break in the continuity of the city's
history. The world in which our Western civilization
made its first appearance towards the end of the seventh
century of the Christian Era was a rural, agricultural
world, not the urban world in which Christianity had
originally propagated itself. Remnants of that urban
world survived only in the Levant, beyond Western
Christendom's southeastern limits.

And then think of the first great battle that the Chris-

tian Church had fought, the battle that it had fought
under the Roman Empire against the worship of collective human power symbolized in the goddess Rome
and the god Caesar. That battle had been fought and
won centuries before our Western civilization first came
into view. And think, too, of the encounter of Christianity with Greek culture, with Greek philosophy, and of
the effect of that intellectual encounter: the formulation
of Christian beliefs in the creeds, the translation of the
Christian faith into the technical terms of Ancient Greek
philosophy. All this had happened before our Western
civilization was heard of or thought of. In fact, the
great events in the history of Christianity, the formative
events that have given Christianity the shape in which
we know it today, had all taken place before the birth of
our Western civilization.

Next let me recall a point that I mentioned in the preceding chapter. Christianity has not been confined within
the limits of our Western society at any stage of the
Christian Church's history; it has always had followers
among non-Western peoples as well. There are the Eastern Orthodox Christians, for example. They are most
numerous today in Russia, and Russia was originally
evangelized by Eastern Orthodox Christians from Southeastern Europe and Asia Minor and Transcaucasia.
There are also the Monophysite Christians, who survive
today in greatest numbers in Abyssinia. The Mono-
physites once extended southwards all the way up the

Nile Valley from Egypt inclusive, and also northwards
from Egypt into Syria and Armenia. And then there are
the Nestorian Christians on the East. The Nestorians
once extended right across Asia: by about the middle of
the seventh century, before the first emergence of our
Western civilization at the western extremity of the
Old World, the Nestorian form of Christianity had
spread all the way across Asia to Northern China. One
of the earliest surviving monuments of the Nestorian
Church in China comes from the city of Si-ngan, in the
present Chinese province of Shensi, which was the capital of China under the T'ang Dynasty. The Nestorians
also extended as far south as the southern tip of India.

There was a moment in the thirteenth century of the
Christian Era when it looked as if the future of Christendom lay with the Nestorian Christians and not with the
Western Christians; for, towards the end of the twelfth
century and the beginning of the thirteenth, there
suddenly came into existence the biggest empire that
has been known to history yet: the empire of the
Mongols. The Mongols were a rather uncivilized, though
militarily efficient, conquering people. In order to orga-
nize their empire, they needed literate secretaries and
clerks and they recruited their clerical staff from among
the Nestorian Christians of Central Asia and Northern
China. Some of the wives of the leading Mongol princes
were also Nestorian Christians; and for a moment it
looked as if Nestorian Christianity might convert the

Mongols and so become the leading branch of Christianity in the World. That possibility rapidly faded away, but it was not the last of the surprising turns of fortune that have been experienced by the Nestorian Church. In our own lifetime the house-painting trade in Chicago has become a preserve of the Nestorian Christians; and, in consequence, has become the principal source of the Nestorian Church's revenue. Administrations gravitate towards the place from which their revenue comes; and today the Patriarch of all the Nestorian Christians of the world, who used to live in Kurdistan, has his residence in Chicago and administers the world-wide Nestorian Christian Church from that centrally situated North American city.

You will have taken my point that Christianity has never been a monopoly of the Western Christians; and I think we may also confidently predict that Christianity will continue to be a living spiritual force in the World for thousands of years after our Western civilization has passed away. Though our vista of history is rather short up to date—extending back, as it does, over no more than a few thousand years—it is already long enough for us to see that all secular institutions, whether they are states or nations or governments or languages or civilizations, have comparatively short lives compared with religions. We can be sure that the Western civilization's role in history is going to be a minor one compared with the role of Christianity.

Christianity has done many incidental things in the World in the course of pursuing its major objectives, and one of its incidental activities has been to serve as a midwife for our Western civilization. The birth of a new civilization in the derelict western provinces of the Roman Empire was a surprising *tour de force*. The western basin of the Mediterranean and the adjacent parts of Western Europe had been brought into the circle of the Graeco-Roman civilization very late in the day, only just before the beginning of the Christian Era, at a date when the Graeco-Roman civilization was already far gone in its decline; so it was natural that the first place where this declining civilization collapsed and caved in should have been this outlying and backward western colonial area. Because we ourselves happen to be Westerners, and because the western part of the Roman Empire therefore happens to be our historical background, we think of the collapse of the Roman Empire in the West as if it had been the collapse of the Roman Empire as a whole. From our parochial standpoint, it looks to us like a supreme catastrophe. It was indeed catastrophic for inhabitants of the Empire who, like Saint Augustine, happened to be domiciled in the western provinces. But, if, by an effort of imagination, we can take ourselves back into the fifth century of the Christian Era, back to the time when the Roman Empire, and the Graeco-Roman civilization with it, was falling in the West, and if we can manage to look at that catastrophe, not through the eyes of some Latin-speaking citizen of North Africa or Gaul or Italy, but through the eyes of someone living at that time in the heart of the Graeco-Roman World, say in Constantinople or in Asia Minor or in Egypt, we shall see the catastrophe in the West in a different light. The news that law and order and civilization were collapsing in the fringe of half-reclaimed territories in the West must have been painful and disturbing; but the reaction to this news in the mind of an inhabitant of Constantinople or of Alexandria will have been: "That is too bad—yet, after all, civilization is still going strong here in the heart of the civilized world. It is a pity that it should have collapsed on the fringes, but we need not take that too tragically, so long as, in the heart, all still goes well."

We can infer this reaction by analogy with our own feelings, in our own time, about the loss, whether permanent or temporary, of the eastern fringes of our modern Western World. I am thinking of the fate of three East-European Occidental countries, Poland, Czechoslovakia, and Hungary, which, since the end of the Second World War, have been under Russian domination. The loss of those eastern fringes of our modern Western World has been painful for us. We should like to liberate and recover those lost provinces of our world if we could. At the same time, we do not feel that the loss of that eastern outer fringe of our world has brought civilization to an end in the heart of our world. We do not even feel that the loss has dealt our civilization a crippling blow. This present reaction of ours throws light on the reaction, in the central and eastern parts of the Roman Empire, to the fall of the Roman Empire in the fifth century of the Christian Era. And we can also surmise that, after the Empire had fallen in the backward West, an observer domiciled in the heart of the Graeco-Roman World would not have foreseen that a new civilization was going to grow up in that derelict western wasteland. Yet, only a few hundred years after the fall of the Roman Empire in the West, a new civilization was beginning to arise there; and this astonishing event surely could not have happened if the Christian Church had not established itself in the Roman Empire's western provinces, as well as in the Empire's heartland, before the Empire fell in the West.

When we look back into the origins of our Western civilization, we find ourselves in the presence of half-a-dozen great men who were heirs of the Graeco-Roman civilization and who at the same time played great parts in the history of the Church. I am thinking of Saint Ambrose, who was the son of a Roman imperial official, and started his own career as an imperial official, till, un-expectedly and to his dismay, he was "drafted" by the people of Milan to become their bishop. I am thinking of Saint Augustine, who started as a professor of Latin literature and migrated from Africa to Milan before he became a Christian bishop in his African homeland. I am thinking of Gregory the Great, who was "city-manager" of Rome at one of the worst moments in the city's history in the sixth century before he became a Benedictine monk and eventually pope. And I am thinking, above all, of Saint Benedict. His parents tried to give him the traditional, conventional Graeco-Roman literary education; but Benedict struck out for himself quite a different line, first as an anchorite and afterwards as the founder and abbot of the earliest Benedictine monastery, which became the mother-house and model for all the Benedictine monasteries that have since been planted throughout the Western World.

The lives of these great men testify that our Western civilization could not have come to birth without the aid of the Christian Church. At the same time there are some key elements in this Western civilization of ours that are not Christian in origin, and there are others that are Christian in origin but that have been de-Christianized in the course of time. The tradition of politics and war in our Western society is not of Christian origin; and here one can detect a difference between the social history of Christianity and that of its two sister religions, Judaism and Islam. Unlike Islam and Judaism, Christianity started on its career in this World in conditions in which the members, and even the leaders, of the early Christian Church found themselves remote from politics. The Church grew up under the Roman Peace. It was automatically protected by the Roman Peace; and the people among whom it originally spread were in walks of life in which they had little political power and no hand at all in military affairs. In fact, as far as one can make out, the attitude of the early Christian Church towards the army and military service and war was not unlike that of the Society of Friends in our Western World in modern times. The early Church did not countenance the enlistment in the army of anyone who was already one of the Church's own members. If an enlisted soldier became a convert to Christianity during his period of service, the Church seems usually to have winked at his remaining in the army until his period of service expired, because the consequences of trying to retire from the army in advance of the stipulated date on the grounds of religious scruple would have been extremely serious for the serving soldier. In general, however, the early Church discountenanced military service and war. So the tradition of politics and war in our Western World is not derived from Christianity. It is derived partly from the Roman Empire, and perhaps more from the war-bands of North-European barbarians who overran the Empire's western provinces in the fifth century. After all, every Western state now existing, not only on the eastern side of the Atlantic but on the western side of it too, is indirectly descended from one or other of the barbarian successor-states of the Roman Empire that were carved out of the western provinces by barbarian war-lords.

There is also a third source of the modern Western attitude towards politics and war, and that is Ancient Greece. When we speak of "the Renaissance," we are usually thinking of the artistic renaissance or the literary renaissance or the architectural renaissance of something from the Ancient Greek civilization. We are less fully aware, I think, of the political renaissance of the ancient Greek World, yet this political manifestation of the Renaissance has had a more lasting effect, and, I should say, also a more unfortunate effect, in our Western World than the renaissance of Greek art and architecture and literature. The political renaissance of Ancient Greece has been effective because we have partly been unconscious of it and partly have flinched from recognizing its influence upon us. The Greek attitude towards the local city-states of the Greek World was one of worship. These states were the true gods of the Ancient Greek World, and the Greeks were conscious of what they were doing and frank in acknowledging it. They consciously symbolized their worship of their city-states by presenting these in the form of goddesses. The collective power of Athens was worshipped by the Athenians in the form of the goddess Athênê, the Guardian of the Citadel; the collective power of Sparta was worshipped by the Spartans in the form of the goddess Athânâ of the Brazen House; and so on in every Greek city-state. In the renaissance of Hellenism in the modern Western World in the fifteenth and sixteenth centuries, this Greek idolatrous attitude towards one's own country, one's own fatherland, was imported from the Ancient Greek past back into our modern Western life. Only, unlike the Greeks, we have flinched from openly admitting that we are practicing this form of idolatry; and consequently we are even more at the mercy of this idolatrous type of Nationalism than the Greeks were at the mercy of their more frankly avowed idolatrous worship of their local states. The Christian Church in the West has had to put up with Western politics and war, those non-Christian elements that have always been part and parcel of our Western life. The Church has sometimes condoned them; it has sometimes tried to redeem them; but it did not originate them, and it has had little influence on them on the whole.

On the other hand, the Christian Church in the West did originate our Western economy. The whole vast economic development of our Western civilization might be regarded by the historian as a by-product of the way of life of the Benedictine Order of Western Christian monks. When Saint Benedict dictated his Rule for his monks, he prescribed a certain amount of work, both manual work and intellectual work, not for its own sake but for the effect that it would have in helping them to lead the spiritual life. And, just because this Benedictine economic work was not an end in itself, but was an incidental means to a spiritual end, it was enormously successful in the economic field as well as in the spiritual field. It succeeded—where the Roman Empire had failed again and again—in restoring agriculture, first in Italy and afterwards in Northern Europe, which the Roman Empire had never conquered or ruled. But this very success in the economic field proved fatal, in the end, to the

Benedictine Order's spiritual purpose. If one jumps from
the Dark Ages to the thirteenth century, and looks at
the lives of the monastic communities at that stage in our
Western history, one finds that, by that time, the enormous success, expansion, and elaboration of the economic
side of the monastaries' activities was diverting a greater
and greater part of the time of a greater and greater number of the monks from the spiritual life to secular busi-
ness. That was the true downfall of the monastic life in
Western Europe, though this choking of the seed by the
cares of the World was happening several hundred years
before the actual dissolution of the monasteries. I call it
the true fall because it was the inner fall in the spiritual
life of the monks themselves, and also because it was this
that lost them the sympathy and affection and support of
the laity. If, in the sixteenth century, the laity had still
felt for the monastic foundations the sympathy and
loyalty that they had felt for them in the eighth and the
ninth and the tenth centuries, no local secular government would have ventured to try to dissolve them. It was
possible to dissolve and plunder the monasteries in the
sixteenth century because they had lost public support,
and they had lost public support because the thorns of
their exuberant economic life had choked the spiritual
life to which their economic activities had been intended
to be subordinate. The enormous economic expansion of
the monasteries excited the covetousness of the laity;
and, when the monasteries were rich and were also dis-

credited, it was easy for the lay powers to plunder them and usurp their economic heritage.

I have mentioned that the Christian Church has made more than one attempt to redeem the non-Christian elements in our Western life. I suppose the greatest and most imaginative attempt to do this, up to date, has been the attempt, beginning in the eleventh century, to make the Papacy the mainspring of a movement for establishing what one might call "the mediaeval Western Commonwealth." Here was a society living in barbarous anarchy. Could the Christian Church in the midst of this society do anything to redeem it? The Papacy set itself in the eleventh century to fight physical anarchy in the Western World with non-material weapons. It had two effective weapons which it set itself to use. One was its unity. The secular world in Western Christendom in the early Middle Ages was divided up among innumerable kingdoms and principalities and city-states. The Church was a unity, it was ecumenical, it was the same Church throughout the whole of Western Christendom. The Church was one; the secular powers were many. That was one source of the Church's strength in trying to bring the lay world into some kind of order without the use of material force. Another of the Church's spiritual weapons was the hold that the Church had on the allegiance of the laity. This hold was so strong that, if the local ruler came into collision with the Church, he had reason to fear that he might not retain the loyalty of his own secular subjects. It was likely that, if they had to choose between their loyalty to the Church and their loyalty to the local prince, they would choose their loyalty to the Church; and this prospect would induce the local ruler to come to terms with the Church before his people deserted him.

The outcome of that early mediaeval experiment depended on whether the mediaeval Western Church could rise to such spiritual heights. To resist the temptation to oppose force with force, it would have to draw its inspiration from the Christian vision of God as being love, and to reject the Christian vision of God as being a jealous God. In our own time we have seen a movement, not in Christendom but in India, led by a great Hindu statesman-saint who, besides his Hindu inspiration, had a Christian inspiration which he acknowledged and which his Hindu followers recognized without ceasing to follow him on that account. The Mahatma Gandhi, like the mediaeval Papacy, opposed a secular power with non-material weapons, and he was more successful in keeping single-mindedly to the use of non-violent weapons only, and in resisting the temptation to retort to force with force. At the critical stage in the same great experiment in mediaeval Western Christendom, Saint Francis of Assisi, the greatest soul that has yet appeared in our Western World, rose to the same heights as the Mahatma Gandhi. But Saint Francis did not become pope, and would not, I suppose, have been a successful pope if he had been elected to the office. When his Order increased in numbers and importance faster than anyone could have expected, he found it not only difficult but excruciating to try to cope with the consequent problems of administration; and in his own lifetime the administration of the Franciscan Order passed into the hands of brothers who brought it into some odium. I am thinking of Brother Elias, who built the beautiful church at the foot of the city of Assisi. By Saint Francis's time, the Papacy had already fallen into the hands of ecclesiastical lawyers, and these brought the ideal of the papal Christian commonwealth into discredit by lapsing into meeting force with physical force in their war of the knife against the Holy Roman Emperor Frederick II and his heirs.

From the later part of the thirteenth century onwards over a period of some four hundred years, the Christian Church in the West went through a very militant chapter of its history; and, in the course of those four hundred years, it became a source of hatred and strife instead of being the source of love and unity which it had aspired and intended to be. The political and military triumph of the Papacy over the Holy Roman Empire was immediately followed by the Papacy's falling under the dominion of another local secular power, the Crown of France, in the so-called Babylonish captivity at Avignon; and the return to Rome was followed by the Great Schism, which was brought about by a nationalistic contest for the control of the Papacy between the Italian cardinals and the French cardinals. The Great Schism was not healed by the Conciliar Movement, which tried but failed to put the government of the Church in Western Christendom on something like a representative federal basis. The papal autocracy was able to defeat that attempt, but was not able to prevent the outbreak of the Reformation, which was the nemesis of the Conciliar Movement's failure. The Reformation was followed by our Western Protestant-Catholic Wars of Religion, and the eventual consequence of this long series of scandals in the history of the Christian Church in the West was a progressive reaction in the West, first against the Papacy, then against the Catholic Church, and then against Christianity itself.

To many of us Westerners in our time, the Western Wars of Religion seem like something that we have now left so far behind us that we cannot imagine its having any bearing on our present life. The Wars of Religion look like that to present-day West Europeans, and to present-day North Americans *à fortiori*. Yet, unless we can bring ourselves to realize that the Wars of Religion and the reaction against them are still active forces in our world in our day, we cannot fully understand the position in which we now find ourselves in our own generation. No battle in the Wars of Religion was fought on American soil. At the same time the Wars of Religion, like other outbreaks of persecution and intolerance, produced a number of "displaced persons," as we call them euphemistically today; and some of those seventeenth-century "displaced persons" were the founders of states of the Union which have played a leading part in American history. The founders of the states of Massachusetts and Connecticut were Congregationalist "displaced persons" taking refuge from Episcopalian persecution in the Old World. The founders of Rhode Island were Quaker "displaced persons" taking refuge from Congregationalist persecution in the New World. Pennsylvania, too, was a Quaker foundation, and the founders of Maryland were Roman Catholic "displaced persons" taking refuge from Protestant persecution. Those five states that came into existence as by-products of the Wars of Religion have played a prominent part in the history of the American people. But, when I say that the reaction against the Wars of Religion is still with us today, I am not thinking in those political terms; I am thinking of the temper which the shock of the Wars of Religion produced in our Western World.

Among the leading spirits in the Western World towards the close of the seventeenth century there was a deliberate transfer of spiritual treasure from religious controversy to the promotion of science and to its application for use in technology. This was a deliberate act of policy. During the Wars of Religion, religious controversy had proved to be a source of hatred and malice and uncharitableness, whereas, in the seventeenth century, science and technology were thought to be possibly useful and certainly harmless. During these last two hundred and fifty years, this secularizing movement has spread through wider and wider circles of our Western society, but unhappily the aims and hopes and expectations of the seventeenth-century fathers of the movement have not been fulfilled. Most of the originators of the movement wanted, not to kill religion, but to salvage religion by liberating it from the fanaticism that had rightly brought it into discredit. In the year 1666 a history of the Royal Society was published in London by an Anglican clergyman named Sprat who was the Society's secretary. The Royal Society was one of the earliest scientific societies to be founded in the English-speaking part of the Western World, and in Sprat's book you will find an interesting account of this society's origin. After the Civil War in England, a number of moderate-minded people were tormented by the political and theological hatred and rancor which had accompanied the Civil War, and they also felt oppressed by the tyranny of the military government which had unexpectedly established itself after the overthrow of the royal power; so they gathered together in Oxford, to take shelter there from the storms of contemporary political and religious life. Many of them were people of keen intelligence. They did not want to let their minds rust; but they had a horror of theological and political discussion, because they felt that this was what had bred all the mischief. They therefore applied themselves to the study and discussion of physical nature. They felt that this was a field in which is was possible to ascertain facts, a field in which there were no political or theological parties, a field in which agreement could be reached on the basis of demonstration and experiment, and, above all, a field in which no ill feelings would be aroused. This Oxford group of students of science was formally constituted into the Royal Society after the restoration of the Monarchy.

The Society's secretary and first historian, Sprat, was not only a clergyman of the Church of England; he eventually rose to be a bishop; and he and those who felt as he did were in no sense anti-Christian or anti-religious. Their calculation was that, if only public interest could be diverted from theology to technology, the temper of the Western World might perhaps cool down to a degree at which it would become possible once again to be religious-minded without being intolerant. Unhappily this calculation turned out to be erroneous. The attack against religious fanaticism passed over in the eighteenth century into an attack on religion itself; and in the twentieth century we have found that religion has been weakened in the West by the West's spiritual history during the last two hundred years, but that fanaticism has not been eradicated. During the eighteenth century and the nineteenth century it looked as if fanaticism had been banished forever from our Western life. Any reasonable common-sense observer in the Western World in those centuries would have said that fanaticism, at any rate, was an enemy of Civilization that had now been extirpated. But we in our time know that fanaticism had not even been banished, but had merely gone underground until it could find a new object to which it could attach itself. In the twentieth century, fanaticism has come back into our life, animating, this time, not our ancestral Western Christianity but our twentieth-century Western ideologies, Nationalism and Communism.

The ideologies claim that, whereas Christianity is old and outworn, they are new and have a mission to fulfil in our time. In truth, however, the ideologies are merely new variations on a very old religion, the religion of man-worship, the worship of collective human power, which is an older religion than Christianity and was, in fact, in the Roman Empire, Christianity's earliest adversary. Communism is a worship of collective human power on a world-wide scale, and in this respect it is a modern counterpart of the worship of the goddess Rome and the god Caesar. Nationalism is a worship of collective human power within local limits, and in this respect it is a modern counterpart of the worship of Athens and Sparta and the other city-states of the Graeco-Roman World before the foundation of the Roman Empire. Man-worship proved to be evil and destructive in its pre-Christian manifestation, but in its present revival its capacity for evil is evidently greater, because it is now armed with new and terrible weapons. We are familiar today with the new physical weapon with which modern

Western fanaticism is armed. This weapon is the modern technology which has been forged by our Western society in the course of the two hundred and fifty years during which it has been devoting itself to technology instead of to religion as its major interest in life. But technology, in itself, is neutral. It is just physical power which can be used for good or for evil, but which is neither good nor evil until human beings employ it for the one purpose or for the other. The more formidable of the two new weapons that the old religion of man-worship now has at its command is the spiritual weapon of fanaticism; and this I should say, though I am conscious that here I am saying something controversial and contentious, is a spiritual weapon that has been forged by the Judaic religions—Judaism, Christianity, and Islam —for any other religion to pick up and use. We are sensitive in the Western World to the use of fanaticism in the cause of Communism. But, on the principle of looking at the beam in one's own eye as well as at the mote in one's brother's eye, it is perhaps more useful for us to consider the effects of fanaticism upon our own form of man-worship, which is not Communism, but Nationalism.

In any part of the Western World today, one may be confronted with the spectacle of the local national flag —a symbol of the idolatrous worship of some local state —being carried into a Christian church, and sometimes one even sees the Cross and a national flag being carried in church in the same procession. Whenever I see that,

I find myself filled with foreboding. Here are two rival religions: traditional Christianity and neo-paganism. They are irreconcilable with one another, and each of them is armed with the formidable force of a fanaticism derived from the Christian and the Jewish past. In the inevitable future war to the death between them, which of them is going to win? Here are their symbols, side by side, being borne aloft, with an apparently equal veneration, within the walls of the same consecrated building. For how long can they continue to co-exist?

In our day Christianity and all the other living higher religions find themselves confronted by a common adversary, the old religion of man-worship in the form of the worship of collective human power. This Nationalist-Communist ideology is animated by Jewish-Christian-Muslim fanaticism; it is equipped with modern Western technology; and it challenges that enormously important negative article of faith that is common to all the higher religions: the conviction that Man is not the greatest spiritual presence in the Universe, but that there is a greater presence—God or absolute reality—and that the true end of Man is to place himself in harmony with this. By comparison with this fundamental issue on which all the living higher religions find themselves on the same side, the issues that divide them seem secondary. In these grave circumstances, ought we not to consider whether the higher religions should not subordinate their differences with one another and stand together against their common adversary? No doubt, we cannot subordinate our convictions. If one drops one's convictions, one cannot stand either singly or collectively. I am not suggesting that the higher religions should drop their respective convictions. To do that would be an act of spiritual self-disarmament. But I do suggest—and this will be the subject of the last chapter in this book—that to retain one's convictions is not incompatible with abandoning a traditional attitude of rivalry and hostility towards people whose convictions differ from one's own. This change of attitude cannot be achieved without a hard struggle; for, in the hearts of all the adherents of all the higher religions, their traditional rivalry and hostility towards one another has become a deeply ingrained habit. If you were to ask a Muslim who was Islam's "enemy number one," the first word that would come to his lips, I suppose, would be "Christianity," not "Communism" or "Nationalism." And if you were to ask a Christian who was Christianity's "enemy number one," "Islam," not "Communism" or "Nationalism," would have been the traditional answer. Communism and Nationalism are, both of them, very new; the feud between Islam and Christianity is rather old; and ingrained habits of attitude and feeling are difficult to change. Can we find a new approach to one another? And, if we can, along what lines of feeling and thought and action can we find it? That is the subject of the fourth and last and most contentious and controversial chapter in this book.

IV

What Should Be the Christian Approach to the Contemporary Non-Christian Faiths?

I HAVE suggested that, in the unified world that has been called into existence by the world-wide expansion of the post-Christian modern Western civilization, all the living higher religions ought to subordinate their traditional rivalries and make a new approach towards one another in face of a fearful common adversary: a revival of the worship of collective human power, armed with new weapons, both material and spiritual. I have also suggested that we might consider whether this reconciliation can be achieved without abandoning convictions, because, without convictions, a religion has no spiritual power.

If the great religions of the World are to approach one another, they must find common ground, and I believe that the necessary common ground exists. The most important piece of common ground is one that has always been there since Mankind first came into existence. This permanent common ground is human nature, especially the self-centeredness which is the Original Sin in human nature. The call to wrestle with Original Sin is the challenge in response to which all the higher religions have arisen. The positive response to this challenge has been very different in each case, but all the religions are grappling with the same problem; and it can hardly be an accident that, as has been pointed out in recent years, the higher religions, as we know them today, all made their appearance in the World within a certain period of time, within something less than a thousand years of one another. They all made their appearance after Original Sin had shown its power by causing the downfall of one or two generations of secular civilizations. In other words, the higher religions appeared at a moment when Mankind had received surprising and humiliating setbacks in its endeavors. These setbacks opened the way for humility, and humility opens the way for spiritual illumination.

For practical purposes, human nature can be taken as being uniform and permanent. It is, of course, true that every individual human soul is in one sense unique and different from every other. It is also true that, within the general framework of psychological uniformity, a number of different psychological types have been identified by present-day schools of psychologists. But these psychological types seem to be distributed equally among all races, and the differences of individual character also cut across all differences of race. So, in a broad way, we may take human nature as being uniform, and we may also take it as being permanent. Theoretically, no doubt, human nature is in process of changing. If we believe that

Man was generated from some prehuman species of creature, it seems possible that he may be evolving into some
other species of creature. But, if there has been any
change since the rise of the first civilizations about five
thousand years ago, this change has been so slight as to
be imperceptible; and the period of time with which
we are concerned in considering the living higher religions is even less than five thousand years. These religions entered the stage of history about two thousand
years after the dawn of the earliest civilizations; and
within these last two or three thousand years the change
in human nature, if there has been any change at all, has
been infinitesimal. The human nature with which we have
to grapple in our own lives today is the same human
nature that evoked the higher religions two or three
thousand years ago. So the higher religions have common
ground in the permanence and universality of human
nature. They have a further piece of common ground in
the present state of the World.

The unification of the World by the modern Western
civilization has confronted all the living higher religions
with a special set of common problems. We have re-
viewed them already, but it may be convenient to re-
capitulate them. First there is "the annihilation of distance" by modern Western technology. This has converted all local problems into world-wide problems. It
is true that human nature has always been uniform.
Original Sin has always been carried by Mankind

wherever Mankind has spread. But, till recently, the consequences of Original Sin might work themselves out locally in one part of the World without affecting other parts. Today we are all of us one another's keepers in the sense that any effect produced by Original Sin in any one part of the World immediately affects the rest of the human race. This is a new situation that has been produced by "the annihilation of distance." Then the replacement of Christianity by technology, as Western Man's foremost concern, has allowed the worship of collective human power to reassert itself, this time armed by technology and animated by Jewish and Christian fanaticism. And then, again, there are the effects of the emancipation movement that has been set in motion today all over the World by the diffusion of modern Western ideals.

All the higher religions are having to come to grips with this movement of emancipation; and, as I suggested in the second chapter, this notion of emancipation is an ambiguous one. There is a movement for the emancipation of power-combines which flows from the worship of collective human power; and there is also a movement for the emancipation of formerly penalized classes of individuals—women, industrial workers, peasants, "natives"—which flows from the worship of the pursuit of individual happiness. The emancipation of "Leviathan" is contrary to everything for which Christianity and the other higher religions stand. Higher religions and "Leviathan" cannot co-exist permanently. On the other hand, the movement for the emancipation of individuals could be redeemed by being reconsecrated. The worshippers of "Leviathan," whether they are Fascists, Nazis, or Communists, jeer at the liberal democratic worshippers of the pursuit of individual happiness. They jeer at them for putting their treasure in such a trivial aim as this; and in truth they have a case, if secular individual happiness is pursued as an end in itself. The attainment of a secular higher standard of living is always unsatisfying, even when this standard is not merely a material one, but includes non-religious spiritual values. But true individual happiness can be pursued and achieved if the aim is to liberate the individual for attaining the true end of Man, which is to glorify God and to enjoy Him forever. To emancipate individual souls in this spiritual sense is the traditional common aim of all the higher religions; and they have all addressed themselves to all men. Each of them has preached a new way of individual salvation, not just to a privileged minority, but to all Mankind without distinction of sex or race or class. So it seems that the higher religions can come to terms with the present world-wide movement for the emancipation of individual souls. It is the higher religions, and they alone, that can give this movement significance and satisfaction by bringing it back to its true spiritual goal; and their greeting to it should be: "I will be your leader." It would be more accurate to say: "I will be your leader again," because this movement for the pursuit of happiness turns out, when one looks back to its historical beginnings, to have had a Christian origin. It has been set in motion by the post-Christian civilization of the modern West, and it is part of the modern West's heritage from its Christian past. Its ultimate inspiration comes from the Christian belief that individual souls have a supreme value for God.

Here there seems to be a possibility of harmonizing all the main movements in the contemporary World except the worship of "Leviathan" in its alternative Nationalist and Communist forms. In this connection, modern Western technology seems to have a constructive and beneficent part to play. It is true that a merely material raising of the standard of living is unsatisfying if pursued as an end in itself. At the same time, it is also true that the spiritual level cannot be raised for Mankind in general unless the material standard is raised for "the depressed classes"—and, today, three-quarters of the human race are still depressed: they are still primitive peasants, living just above the starvation line and often falling below it. A higher level of spiritual life is not ultimately compatible with gross social injustice; and the co-existence, in the past, of saintliness and injustice explains why, hitherto, a voluntary acceptance of poverty has always played so large a part in the experience and life of the saints of all the great religions.

The saints have embraced poverty for more than one

reason: in order to share the common lot of the mass of Mankind, and also in order to extricate themselves from the spiritually demoralising effect of material welfare. This is obviously demoralising when it is the monopoly of a privileged minority, as it always has been in the past. But let us imagine a future state of affairs in which material goods will be in such abundant supply that there will be enough for everyone in the world to have his fill. This picture of the future does not now seem utopian, when we view it in the light of our technological achievements. Yet the example of the mediaeval Western monasteries shows that, when material wealth and efficiency and success increase out of proportion to the sublimation of the spiritual life, they tend to choke and smother the spiritual life and would have the same tendency even if their fruits were justly distributed. For all these reasons, the saints in the past have embraced poverty, and the last-mentioned reason is a permanent reason for embracing poverty if one is seeking the goal of spiritual perfection. In the past the material resources of civilization were not sufficient to bring the amenities of civilization within the reach of more than a small minority of the members of Society; and, in those past conditions, social injustice was perhaps part of the price that had to be paid for civilization. But in our time modern Western technology is making social injustice avoidable, and is therefore making it intolerable. The higher religions all believe in the consecration of human personalities by bringing them into harmony with God or absolute reality, greatly though they differ from one another in their prescriptions for achieving this spiritual result. Social justice—not as an end in itself, but as a means toward the end of glorifying God and enjoying Him—is evidently in harmony with the spiritual purpose of the higher religions. In fact, social justice can be achieved only as a by-product of the achievement of this spiritual purpose that reaches so far beyond it.

This brings us to the question: In the particular social circumstances in which we are living today against the permanent and universal background of human nature with its Original Sin, what must Western Christians do, for their part, in order to meet their brothers, the followers of the other higher religions, on the ground that is common to all of us? This question is confronting all of us today in a world that is rapidly coalescing. I dare say the Congress of the Buddhist World, which recently has been in session in Burma, has been discussing this very question. But, for us in the West, it is more profitable to discuss it from our side. We have to consider the action that *we* should take, the spirit in which *we* should meet our non-Western fellow men.

My first suggestion would be that we in the West should try to purge our Christianity of its Western accessories. Here an admirable example has been set us by the Western Christian missionaries in the earliest wave of Western missionary work in modern times: the Jesuit

missionaries in China and India in the sixteenth and seventeenth centuries. The Jesuits were, of course, highly
cultivated men. They were masters of all the resources of
Western Christendom, which, by that time, was a highly
cultivated civilization. And, when they came upon the
civilizations of China and India, they were able to appre-
ciate the fact that here they were in the presence of great
cultures, which, on the secular side, were built upon different foundations from the Western culture—upon different philosophies, for instance. The Jesuits were not
unmindful of the fact that, in the early centuries of the
life of the Christian Church in the Graeco-Roman
World, the fathers of the Church—especially the
Alexandrian fathers, Clement and Origen, in the second
and early third centuries of the Christian Era—had been
aware of the same problem of having to express Christianity in terms familiar to the people to whom they were
addressing themselves. In that time and place, Christianity
had to be interpreted to people with a Greek philosophical education. The Jesuit missionaries realized that the
Greek terms in which Christianity had been expressed
from the time of the Roman Empire onwards were not
the best terms for making it acceptable to the minds and
the hearts of Chinese and Indians. So they deliberately
set themselves to divest their Christianity of its Western
and its Graeco-Roman accessories and to put it to the
Chinese and the Indians in their own terms.

This operation is one that is necessary at all times, because we are always relapsing from the worship of God into the worship of our tribe or of ourselves; and therefore we Christians, whether we are Western Christians or Eastern Christians, tend to treat Christianity as if it were the tribal religion of our particular civilization. In the West, we tend to treat it as something that is inseparable from the West, and even as something that derives its virtue not so much from being Christian as from being Western. You may remember that, at the time of the negotiation of the Vatican agreements between Mussolini and Pope Pius XI, only a few weeks before the agreements were finally concluded, Mussolini made a characteristic speech in the Italian Senate in which he sounded the praises of the Italian people and glorified their historical achievements. Just think, he said on this occasion, what our Italy has done for a wretched little Oriental sect that started life far away in Palestine, in a remote corner of the Roman Empire where it had no prospects and no influential members. Left to itself, Christianity would have been bound to wither and die away. It was salvaged, thanks to being carried to Rome. There the Italian genius made its fortune, and now it has become the universal Roman Catholic Church of which Italy has the honor to be the center. A week or two later, the Pope addressed a letter to one of his cardinals in which he replied to Mussolini's speech. The scene of Christ's ministry, the Pope pointed out, was not Italy but Palestine; and the Church was universal already in the age of the Apostles when Palestine was still the field of their labors. It was universal in Saint Peter's hands when he was still in Palestine and before he went to Rome. The universality of the Christian Church was independent of its associations with Rome and with Italy. Coming from the mouth of the Pope, the bishop of Rome, this pronouncement was impressive and authoritative. It was a remarkable declaration of the universality of Christianity, and condemnation of any attempt to identify it with one's own city or country or tribe or civilization. Mussolini's account of the history of Christianity was indeed historically untrue, besides being spiritually wrong. In the preceding chapter I have contended that Christianity has always been a gospel not just for the West but for the whole human race, and that there have always been important non-Western Christian churches. If we approach the followers of non-Western Christianity and of the non-Christian higher religions as Christians simply and not as Christian Westerners—if we can distinguish our religion from our civilization—we shall be more likely to succeed in getting on to terms with our neighbors and appealing to both their hearts and their minds.

My next suggestion is more controversial, because it raises a more crucial issue. We ought also, I should say, to try to purge our Christianity of the traditional Christian belief that Christianity is unique. This is not just a Western Christian belief; it is intrinsic to Christianity itself. All the same, I suggest that we have to do this if we are to purge Christianity of the exclusive-mindedness and intolerance that follows from a belief in Christianity's uniqueness.

Here I should like to draw a distinction which, I think, is all-important, though also, no doubt, debatable. I should say that one can be convinced of the essential truth and rightness and value of what one believes to be the fundamental points in one's own religion—and can believe that these tenets have been received by one as a revelation from God—and at the same time not believe that *I, my* church, *my* people, have the sole and unique revelation. If one accepts, and builds on, the Jewish and Christian vision of God as being love, one would feel it unlikely, no doubt, that I and my church and my people had not had *some* revelation from God. If God loves mankind, He would have made a revelation to us among other people. But, on the same ground and in virtue of the same vision of what God's nature is, it would also seem unlikely that He would not have made other revelations to other people as well. And it would seem unlikely that He would not have given His revelation in different forms, with different facets, and to different degrees, according to the difference in the nature of individual souls and in the nature of the local tradition of civilization. I should say that this view is a corollary of the Christian view of God as being love.

Nevertheless, to purge Christianity of its exclusive-mindedness is a much harder task than to purge it of its Western accretions. The vein of exclusiveness and intolerance in Christianity is not, I should say, an especially Western deformation of Christianity; it is a congenital feature which is part of Christianity's and also part of Islam's heritage from Judaism. Just as the vision of God as being love is a heritage from Judaism, so is the other vision of God as being a jealous god, the god of *my* tribe as against the gentiles *outside* my tribe or my church or whatever my community may be. Yet, however hard it may be to purge Christianity of its exclusive-mindedness, it seems imperative for Christians to achieve this spiritual feat, and this for a number of reasons. The paramount reason is that exclusive-mindedness is a sinful state of mind. It is the sin of pride, and we know that the sin of pride is an arch sin, because it is a gateway for the entry of all the other sins, and a roadblock across the path of repentance. The sin of pride is insidious. Its first form is in the first person singular—*I* am self-centered and proud, *I* am egotistic about *my*self; but this is the less insidious of the two forms of the sin, because it is comparatively easy to see through oneself and to perceive that one is not the center of the Universe. The sin of pride becomes mortally dangerous when it is translated from the singular into the plural, from egoism into what, to coin a word, one might call "nosism." I am told that, in Arabic, there is a word for the sin of pride in the collective first person plural. The Arabs call this "nahni-

yah" from the Arabic word "nahnu," meaning "we."
When we are committing the sin of pride in the first person plural, it is easy for us to persuade ouselves that we are not proud of *ourselves*; we are proud of our family, our people, our community, our church. We persuade ourselves that our feeling is not personal to ourselves; yet we do not escape the sin of pride by magnifying it from the singular into the plural. We increase its danger—in the first place because it is easier for us, in this case, to believe that we are not committing it, and in the second place because the sin of pride in the plural has far more material power behind it than the feeble power of any sinful individual.

This sin of pride, especially in the first person plural, is an expression of self-centeredness; and this is another reason for trying to cast it out. As an expression of self-centeredness it is incompatible with the Christian intuition that God is, not self-centered, but just the opposite: self-sacrificing. If God is self-sacrificing, if the Christian vision of God as being self-sacrificing is a true vision, as we believe it to be, then it follows that all we human beings who see that vision and believe it to be the truth should do our best to follow it to the extent of our feeble powers, and therefore should do our best to break out of self-centeredness in the plural as well as in the singular. That would be the only way of putting ourselves in harmony with a god who is not self-centered but is self-sacrificing. And then the historian, surveying the present scene with his eyes looking over his shoulder into the past, would say that in the past this arrogant, intolerant vein in Christianity has in fact led—and, you might even say, has rightly led—to the rejection of Christianity. In the seventeenth century, Christianity was rejected first by the Japanese, then by the Chinese, and finally by the intellectual leaders of the Western World in Western Christendom itself, and in every case for the same reason. The same Christian arrogance, if Christians fail to purge it out of Christianity now, will lead to the rejection of Christianity in the future. If Christianity is presented to people in that traditional arrogant spirit, it will be rejected in the name of the sacredness of human personalities—a truth to which the whole human race is now awakening under the influence of the modern Western civilization, which originally learned that truth from the Christianity that modern Man has been rejecting. Christian arrogance is un-Christian and anti-Christian, and here we seem to be confronted once again with the unresolved conflict—inherited by Christianity and Islam from Judaism—between two visions of the nature of God, two visions which, I believe, are mutually incompatible.

What, then, should be the attitude of contrite Christians toward the other higher religions and their followers? I think that it is possible for us, while holding that our own convictions are true and right, to recognize that, in some measure, all the higher religions are also revelations of what is true and right. They also come from God and each presents some facet of God's truth. They may and do differ in the content and degree of the revelation that has been given to Mankind through them. They may also differ in the extent to which this revelation has been translated by their followers into practice, both individual practice and social practice. But we should recognize that they too are light radiating from the same source from which our own religion derives its spiritual light. This must be so if God is the god of all men and is also another name for love.

We have also to reckon with a point that was brought up in one of the discussions that I had the advantage of having, after one of the lectures on which this book is based, with members of my audience. When one makes comparisons between religions, the great difficulty is that one's relation to the religion in which one has been brought up is very much more intimate than one's relation to other religions which one has learned to know later in life, and therefore, to some extent, from outside. In comparing one's own family religion or ancestral religion with other religions, one is comparing two things to which one's emotional relation is different; and therefore it is difficult to make an objective judgement between them. I think the great difference is that one's feelings about one's own religion, whether they are feelings of assent and love and loyalty or feelings of repudiation and hostility, are inevitably stronger than one's feelings about other religions, whether one's feelings about these other religions are friendly or hostile. When one tries to discount one's special emotional feeling for one's ancestral religion, one is in danger of leaning over backwards and going to the other extreme of rejecting one's own religion rather violently and admiring other religions rather uncritically just because of one's having no such intimate acquaintance with them. One knows one's ancestral religion from inside, for evil as well as for good. I myself am conscious of not feeling so indignant at the crimes committed by Muslim fanaticism as I feel at the crimes committed by Christian fanaticism; and I think this is because those Muslim misdeeds are not part of my own ancestral religious history, and so I do not feel the same responsibility for them that I feel for the misdeeds of the religion and the church in which I myself have been born and brought up.

Here, then, is an obstacle to intercourse between members of different religions. Yet this obstacle cannot be an insuperable one; for, long before the present annihilation of distance by modern Western means of communication, the members of different religions have had meetings and discussions, and there have been conversions from one religion to another. I think we can foresee that, if the world continues to grow together into a single family, objective judgements between different living religions will become in the course of time rather less difficult to make, as the unification of the World pro-

ceeds. I think one form that this unification will take will
be a unification of our different cultural heritages. Christians and Muslims are already familiar with the fact that
the Jewish cultural heritage was, from the beginning, a
part of the Christian and Islamic cultural heritage. I think
one can foresee a time when the heritages of Islam and
Buddhism will also have become part of the Christian
society's background. The heritage of Christianity always has been, to some extent, a part of the Islamic
society's background. One might also foresee its becoming part of the Buddhist society's background. And in
our time already we have seen how the Christian heritage
did become part of the background of a great Hindu
saint, the Mahatma Gandhi. We have seen how Gandhiji
held the allegiance of the whole Hindu World, though
his Hinduism was obviously tinged and blended with elements of Christianity which he himself did not disown.
And we have seen the immense effect on the World of
this two-fold religious inspiration harmonized in one
great soul.

On a less exalted plane than Gandhi's we already see
Christians of ordinary spiritual stature making individual
choices in grown-up life between the Protestant and the
Catholic versions of Western Christianity and between
the Western and non-Western versions of Christianity.
This exercise of free choice has given birth to Roman
Catholic Uniate Churches composed of Christians who
are ex-Eastern Orthodox or ex-Monophysite or ex-Nes-

torian; and the Protestant Western Churches, too, have
their converts from non-Western Churches. Both the
Protestant Western Churches and the Catholic Western
Church also have converts from Hinduism and Buddhism
and Confucianism, as well as from the primitive religions. It is true that converts to Christianity from
Judaism are less common, and converts to Christianity
from Islam are very rare indeed; but, on the whole, I
think we can already see a tendency for people to pass
by deliberate choice from one religion to another, in
contrast to the traditional state of religious affairs in
which, almost automatically one remained for life in the
religious communion into which one had been intro-
duced by the accident of being born in a particular place
at a particular time. I think this tendency towards making a free choice of religion in grown-up life is likely to
increase as the World grows closer together.

In the light of history I should not expect to see mankind converted to a "syncretistic" religion, constructed
artificially out of elements taken from all the existing
religions. Such artificial religions have been, and are
being, manufactured; but I should not expect to see any
of them capture the imagination and the feelings and the
allegiance of Mankind. I should not expect this because
such attempts are generally made only partly for religious
reasons, and partly for utilitarian reasons which are other
than religious. I am thinking of attempts in the past like
the Mughal emperor Akbar's attempt in India, in the

early years of the seventeenth century, to create a new
composite religion blending elements of Islam and Hinduism and Zoroastrianism and Christianity; or the attempt
of the Roman Emperor Julian to reverse the triumph of
Christianity in the Roman Empire by building up artificially a pagan counter-church in which he tried to weld
together all the non-Christian religions in the Roman Empire. It is notorious that such attempts have failed in the
past, and I think they are also likely to fail in the future,
as far as the past is any guide to the future. At the same
time, when I find myself in Chicago and when, travelling
northwards out of the city, I pass the Bahai temple there,
I feel that in some sense this beautiful building may be a
portent of the future. I suppose the Chicagoan Bahais are
mostly converts from Christianity. It is true that one
can become a convert to Bahaism with a minimum of dis-
turbance of one's ancestral religious roots. Of all the
Judaic religions, Bahaism is the most tolerant. In its
catholicity, it comes near to Mahayanian Buddhism or
to Hinduism. I would not say that I expect to see a
coalescence of the historic religions, but I think it may be
expected, and also may be hoped, that all religions, while
retaining their historic identities, will become more and
more open-minded, and (what is more important) open-
hearted, towards one another as the World's different
cultural and spiritual heritages become, in increasing
measure, the common possession of all Mankind. I should
say that, in learning more and more to respect, reverence,
admire, and love other faiths, we should be making prog-

ress in the true practice of Christianity. And the practice of the Christian virtue of charity need not prevent us from holding fast to what we believe to be the essential truths and ideals in our own Christian faith.

Here we come to a point of capital importance which is also a high controversial one. I think we can and should continue to preach these truths and ideals to the non-Christian majority of our fellow human beings, and, when I say preach, I am using the word in the most inclusive sense, to include not merely expounding Christianity by word, but also giving practical examples of it in action. One can see, from what has happened in the past, that, in winning people's assent and allegiance and devotion, action has always counted, and rightly counted, for far more than words. The death of one martyr will probably have more effect, illogical though this may seem, than volumes and volumes of the most competent theological exposition of the solitary martyr's faith. If we can express what we believe to be the essential truths and precepts of our own religion in action as well as in words, and if at the same time we can be receptive to the truths and ideals of the other faiths, we shall be more likely to win the attention and good will of the followers of those other faiths. If we can learn to present Christianity in this spirit, we can perhaps manage to present it with conviction without at the same time relapsing into Christianity's traditional sin of arrogance and intolerance.

I have spoken of "essential elements" in Christianity

and other religions, and this compels me to declare what I myself consider to be the essential elements in Christianity. One attempts this at one's peril, but in writing this book I should not be doing my duty if I did not make the attempt. So, with great diffidence, I will pick out three points in Christianity which seem to me to be essential. The first point is that Christianity has a vision of God as loving His creatures so greatly that He has sacrificed Himself for their salvation. The essence of this vision is conveyed in four verses of the second chapter of Saint Paul's Epistle to the Philippians. In the King James version at least one of the sentences in that passage has been mistranslated in a way that misrepresents the meaning. I should translate the passage like this:

"The spirit that you should have is the spirit that was in Christ Jesus. There He was in the form of God, yet He did not take being on an equality with God as a prize to be clutched. No, He emptied Himself by assuming the form of a servant, taking on a human guise. But He did not only expose Himself in human shape; He humbled Himself by being submissive to the extent of submitting to die, and this by a death on the cross."

I feel that this passage sums up the first essential point in Christianity. The second essential point would be a conviction that human beings ought to follow the example that God has set them in His incarnation and crucifixion. And the third point would be not just to hold this conviction theoretically but to act on it as far as one is able. Here the gap between the Christian ideal and Christian performance has been, as we all recognize, enormous. But this *is* the Christian ideal; and it is impossible to profess Christianity without knowing that this is its ideal and without feeling a call from Christ to act on it in one's own life as far as one can. I should say that these three points are essential in Christianity, but I should not say that they are exclusively Christian. I think that they have non-Christian precedents in Mankind's past, and also living non-Christian parallels.

Let us think first of the Christian vision of Almighty God as being self-sacrificing. Is not that a Christian heritage from nature-worship? Does it not come, at any rate historically speaking, from the vision of a vegetation god, a grain god, a Tammuz or Adonis or Osiris, who sacrifices himself in order to give Man the bread of life? The material bread of life, which those vegetation gods gave to Man at their own cost, is the image that has given us the vision of the spiritual bread of life. And then we have the Christian vision of Christ deliberately divesting Himself of His divine bliss in order to bring salvation to Man. This, I think, has a parallel in the "northern" or "late" or Mahayanian Buddhist vision of the being who in that version of Buddhism is called a bodhisattva. It is an interesting point in the history of Buddhism that, between the birth of the earlier school of Buddhism and the birth of the later school, Buddhism seems, at any rate to an outside observer, to have changed its ideal. I have mentioned that the ideal of the earlier school of Buddhism was to liberate oneself from suffering. This was presented as the paramount aim towards which every sentient creature, human or non-human, should strive. In the later version of Buddhism that ideal has been replaced by one which seems to a Christian observer to have moved in a Christian direction. In this later Buddhism the ideal figure is not the Buddhist ascetic sage who has liberated himself from existence by fighting his way, through rough and strenuous spiritual exertions, into the peace of Nirvana. It is the bodhisattva, a being of the highest spiritual nature known to Man who has fought his way to the threshold of Nirvana, and who then, like the Buddha himself during his forty years on Earth after his enlightenment, has deliberately refrained from entering into his rest in order to remain in this world of suffering. The bodhisattva has voluntarily postponed his self-release for ages and ages (the Buddhists and Hindus reckon in large numbers) in order to show the way of salvation to his fellow beings by helping them along the path on which he himself is refraining, out of love and compassion for them, from taking the last step.

You might perhaps comment: "Well, yes, that is a form of self-sacrifice, but it is a rather unheroic form, is it not, compared with the Christian vision of a god who, instead of just refraining from entering into bliss, deliberately steps out of bliss in order to suffer crucifixion." A comment on this comment might be that every great ideal has its price. When one compares the religions of the Indian school with the religions of the Palestinian school, one might say: "Yes, it is true that the Indian religions are less heroic, but they have also been less atrocious." There have been persecutions and martyrdoms in Eastern Asia as well as in Western Asia and in the Western World, but on the whole the Chinese government was milder in its persecutions of Buddhism than the Roman government or the Protestant and Roman Catholic governments in the modern West have been in their persecutions of Christianity. The ordeals to which the Buddhist martyrs in China were put may have been less severe than those inflicted on the Christian martyrs in the Roman Empire; but then the temperature both of government and of religion has been lower in Eastern Asia both for evil and for good. So I would come back to my point that, in the later Buddhist idea of the bodhisattva, we do have, independently of Christianity, the vision of a self-sacrificing figure. It is not God, but it is a supreme being—a being who has reached the highest point to which sentient creatures can rise.

In the first chapter of the history of Christianity, while Christianity was fighting a spiritual war with man-worship in the form of the worship of the Roman Empire, it was at the same time competing peacefully with a number of religions of its own kind: the worship of the goddess Isis, the worship of the goddess Cybele, and Mithraism. In entering into a charitable competition with another group of sister religions—the other living higher religions of the contemporary world—Christians today can feel sure, in advance, of two things. In a peaceful competition, the best of the competing religions will eventually win the allegiance of the whole human race. If we believe that God is love, we shall also believe that the whole human race will eventually turn to whichever vision of God is the fullest vision and gives the greatest means of grace. We can also forecast that the winning religion, whichever it may be, will not eliminate the other religions that it replaces. Even if it does replace them, it will achieve this by absorbing into itself what is best in them. In winning the competition between the higher religions in the Roman Empire, Christianity did not really eliminate Isis-worship or Cybele-worship or Mithraism. One of the means by which it won, and one of the conditions on which it won, was that it should and did absorb into itself what was valuable in those rival religions. In the ideal of the church militant on Earth one can see the abiding imprint of Mithraism on Christianity. As for the influence of the worships of Isis and Cybele, one sees this in the rather unhappy difference of feeling and opinion and attitude, between Protestants and Nestorians on the one side and Roman Catholics and Eastern Orthodox Christians on the other, over the cult of the Virgin Mary. Now whether that cult is literally descended from Isis-worship or Cybele-worship I do not know. But I think a psychologist would say that it is psychologically associated with their replacement. I think he would say that the vision of the mother goddess has so strong a hold on human nature that it cannot be banished permanently from any religion that is to last for long or is to command the allegiance of great numbers of people. So I imagine that, if I were a Roman Catholic, I should take with equanimity the Protestant strictures on the cult of the Virgin, shocking though in many ways that cult has been, and is, to Protestant feelings.

For these reasons, I believe that Christians today can face the future with confidence if they face it with charity and humility. The crucial point that I want to make is that we can have conviction without fanaticism, we can have belief and action without arrogance or self-centeredness or pride. At the end of the struggle in the Roman Empire between the victorious Christian Church and the local pre-Christian religion, there was a celebrated incident at the time when the Christian Roman imperial government was forcibly closing the pagan temples and suppressing pagan forms of worship in the western part of the Roman Empire. In the course of this campaign the government ordered the removal, from the senate house at Rome, of the statue and altar of Victory which had been placed there by Julius Caesar. The spokesman of the Senate at the time, Quintus Aurelius Symmachus, had a controversy with Saint Ambrose on the subject, and the documents have survived. Symmachus was beaten, not in argument, but by *force majeure*. The government simply closed the temples and removed the statues. But, in one of his last pleas, Symmachus has put on record these words: "It is impossible that so great a mystery should be approached by one road only." The mystery of which he is speaking is the mystery of the Universe, the mystery of Man's encounter with God, the mystery of God's relation to good and evil. Christianity has never answered Symmachus. To suppress a rival religion is not an answer. The question raised by Symmachus is still alive in the World today. I think we shall have to face it in our time.

INDEX